Retail Design

Retail Design
Otto Riewoldt

co-ordinating researcher Jennifer Hudson

 LAURENCE KING

WITHDRAWN
FROM STOCK

Published 2000 by Laurence King Publishing
an imprint of Calmann & King Ltd
71 Great Russell Street
London WC1B 3BP
Tel: +44 20 7831 6351
Fax: +44 20 7831 8356
Email: enquiries@calmann-king.co.uk
www.laurence-king.com

A catalogue for this book is available
from the British Library.

ISBN 1 85669 215 9

Translated from German
by Susan Mackervoy

Designed by Frank Philippin
at brighten the corners

Picture research by Jennifer Hudson
and Susan Lawson

Printed in Hong Kong

Frontispiece: Interior of Advanced Cique
fashion boutique, Tokyo, Japan (see pp 74–9),
photograph by Nacása & Partners

contents

132
shopping as leisure

192

the great comeback

introduction

New approaches to retail design In the plant world, hybrids are an unmistakable sign that the natural order of things has gone awry. A very similar phenomenon is currently observable in the design of retail environments, which is evolving towards the entertainment industry at a rampant pace. Architecture and design have attained a new status in the retail world, where they are called on to create distinctive brand and corporate images. The motivation behind these efforts to create ever more impressive real-life retail experiences is that retailers feel very insecure, indeed threatened, in the face of the virtual alternative, which appears to exercise an overpowering attraction for consumers. This fearsome rival is called e-commerce.

The internet challenge No other technical development has changed the way we handle information, services and goods so rapidly as the internet. This virtual arena for information and communication, scarcely ten years old, encompasses almost all spheres of life and has transformed the ways in which news is disseminated and received, working processes and organizations are structured, and business of all types is originated and transacted.

The rapid pace at which the worldwide web has achieved global acceptance is also without technological precedent. The enormous, irresistible attraction lies in the inherent symbiosis of reception and interaction offered by this

medium. Both local and international information can be accessed on one's screen at home or on mobile electronic devices twenty-four hours a day – and direct action and interaction are just as easy, too. The world has become a 'global village'.

Many everyday, familiar processes are simpler on the internet. This is especially true of purchasing. At the click of a mouse, consumers can survey the full range of products on offer, compare prices more easily than ever before, book holidays, buy and bid for products, and communicate directly about their likes and dislikes with dealers, producers and other customers. And this at any time of the day or night, seven days a week.

Retail under pressure Yet this is not all. Within the retail sector itself things are changing. On the world's stock exchanges, the shares of the major international trading groups are largely stagnant: their day as speculative investments has long since passed. The retail scene is dominated by drastic price wars; in the face of unfavourable socio-demographic trends the cross-border process of concentration and cut-throat competition is in full swing. That this is not a recent crisis is shown by the fate of the large department stores, once so successful: in Germany their market share fell from 10 per cent in 1970 to 5 per cent in 1994; during the same period, hypermarkets, self-service stores and discount chains

saw their market share rise to 12.6 per cent. Another irreversible trend is the polarization of the retail sector: at one end of the spectrum, price-sensitive mass-market goods are piled high in standardized retail formats ('big boxes'); at the other end are the 'retail experiences' designed for pleasure, created to lure consumers into malls and shopping centres.

In the world's highly developed markets, populations are stagnating, older consumers are in the majority and consumer habits are changing. The fact that tourism ranks high on the scale of consumer desires illustrates the general shift from products towards services highlighted by market research experts. In response, one-time full-range operators are now seeking to home in on selected consumer segments by pruning and focusing their range: specialist discount stores are creating internal competition, and department stores are being restyled to focus on women's products – perfumes, cosmetics, lingerie, health/beauty – or as lifestyle warehouses for well-heeled, trend-conscious consumers between the ages of 25 and 45.

New forms of retailing are competing with the traditional operators for a share of the cake of consumers' disposable income – a cake that is unlikely to become significantly larger in the foreseeable future. Business-to-consumer – direct selling from the manufacturer or the brand to the end customer – is not the sole province of e-commerce: via factory outlets, corporate flagship stores, and franchise chains – and in some extreme cases even via manufacturers' own theme parks – customers are increasingly being addressed directly, cutting out the traditional middle man.

Staging happiness In his book entitled *Erlebnisgesellschaft* ['The Experience Society'], internationally renowned sociologist Gerhard Schulze observes: 'Whereas the goals of previous generations were primarily material ones – their own house, their own car – today we define the meaning of our life in psycho-physical terms: what makes me feel good? That is the central question in our contemporary search for meaning.' In his latest publication *Kulissen des Glücks* ['Staging Happiness'] he analyses the various urban or semi-urban settings created to produce these sensations: 'They are consciously constructed façades, which are filled with life by suppliers and consumers. They are there to generate a beautiful experience, a moment of happiness.'

Creating a stage set, an arena for experience, the integration of shopping and entertainment in new, attractive configurations: these are the leitmotifs of the retail sector's counter-offensive against its electronic competition. Only through real-life experience, through an unmediated encounter with the tangible attractions of beautiful things, can it hope to win through against the convenience and efficiency of e-commerce. In their book *The Experience Economy* (1999), authors B. Joseph Pine II and James H. Gilmore argue that: 'Theatre is not a metaphor but a model'. With the same care and professionalism as in the theatre, the sequence of events must be worked out in detail, including everything from props to stage directions, in order to transform the sale of merchandise into an experience-intensive act – one in which the potential customers are actors rather than passive spectators and the happy end is when they reach for their credit card: 'Staging experiences is not about entertaining customers, it's about engaging them'.

Cities rediscovered Whether as spectator or cast member – the public loves change. Consequently, city centres are once again becoming the focus of interest for both investors and consumers, after decades of emigration to the urban peripheries. The new city-centre retail units are much larger than their predecessors, housed in large, centrally located properties which have partially or entirely lost their original function – brand new retail centres are implanted in historic railway buildings, for example, or abandoned factory sites.

Urban ambience has the edge over the cold, sterile splendour of greenfield sites – even in the USA, where the typical American malls are suffering from dwindling visitor numbers and investors are once again setting their sights on the forgotten Main Street. Instead of conjuring up ever more lavish man-made centres, where all the same brands and names are collected together in the conventional glitzy setting, they are transforming deserted high streets into car-free pedestrian zones and creating new high streets following traditional models.

The catchphrase 'urban entertainment centre' encapsulates the spirit of the city-centre revival. On dilapidated or newly-created city blocks, architects are creating gaudily dressed, but morally impeccable entertainment and shopping districts on the model of New York's Times Square. After German reunification, the capital city provided an ideal testing ground for the simulation of inner-city architectural textures: on Berlin's Potsdamer Platz, previously split by the border and the wall, a complete metropolitan district was created within the space of a few years, complete with office towers, theatres, cinema complexes, hotels, a wide range of catering establishments and glass-covered shopping arcades. Not far away, investors put up three interconnected arcades on the Friedrichsstrasse, formerly famous as a bustling shopping street.

Success factor architecture In Berlin, the new Potsdamer Platz instantly became the city's leading tourist attraction and a magnet for admiring shoppers. This is a striking illustration of the general trend towards shopping as a leisure pursuit – and the effectiveness of the architecture as a retail 'stage set' for the experience is a key success factor here. Whether in the city centre, or as an appendage to airports, or as a retail oasis set amidst landscape: to achieve the goal of this new mix of attractions – a larger number of customers, staying for a longer time, and ideally spending more money – the architectural ingredients also have to be right.

Surveys from the USA prove that malls with a high experience/entertainment value achieve an average length of stay of four hours per visitor, while those without score just 60 to 90 minutes. That architecture is among the requisite show effects can be regarded as generally accepted, since department store and supermarket groups have been having their flagship outlets designed by top architects.

In the old world, too, retailers are picking up on traditions of the past. After all, Gustave Eiffel was among the first department store architects, as the designer of Au Bon Marché in Paris, which opened in 1887. In Germany, department store projects by Joseph Maria Olbrich and Erich Mendelsohn marked the emergence of modernism. As late as 1957, Bauhaus legend Marcel Breuer was responsible for the reconstruction of the Bijenkorf department store in Rotterdam, which had been destroyed during the war. After an interlude of several decades, when faceless, functional boxes dominated the scene, these historic traditions began to re-emerge. Among the pioneers was fashion department store chain Peek & Cloppenburg, active across Europe, which commissioned new buildings from architects of international standing including Gottfried Böhm (Berlin, 1995), Moore & Rubble (Leipzig, 1995) and Renzo Piano (Cologne, 2001).

Trendsetting shop designs Retail is a constantly changing business. Along with the leisure industry there is no other segment of the property market that is subject to such short-term variations. Designers of retail interiors and display systems have to develop a telepathic sensitivity to the latest trends in products, markets and customer expectations – or else set the trends themselves, and with the fastest possible effect. Global brands and international retail groups are not immune to rapid changes of style and taste: the over-extension of a brand image and the excessive market presence that is the product of success can pose serious dangers in themselves.

As a result, the dialectic between the recognition factor and the surprise factor in the design of retail spaces and showrooms is becoming increasingly important to ensure a balance between continuity and regeneration. This is how Dutch retail designer Jos de Vries defines the central function of the retail concept: 'The target group must feel at home, must be enthralled by the product range, by the price, the image projected by the personnel or by the ambience in the store, and in so doing its expectations must be exceeded: the wow! factor'. As the direct mediator of the brand experience, the retail spaces must themselves be effectively branded. Right down to the smallest detail, they are designed to communicate a distinctive message and emotional identity. Hardware and soft values are incorporated in subtle, suggestive persuasion strategies that guide visitors through the product world, directing and steering their attention in positively dramatic fashion: 'Lighting, odours, time and temperature have now also become important factors, with the intention of stimulating the customers' purchasing behaviour' (de Vries). The experience mix is often based on inter-changeable, standardized modules that are used in retail outlets and point-of-sale environments worldwide – but this does not matter, as long as the retail environment, as 'visual merchandising', avoids monotony, or is renewed as frequently as the collections themselves.

Learning from the past How long-lasting the projects in this volume prove to be, how many of them will already have been dismantled, converted or redecorated by the time of publication, is not a relevant issue here. This snapshot of the diverse manifestations of present-day retail design is a contribution to the history of design in our contemporary period – whose creations will be just as transient and just as distinctive as the great arcades or department stores of the nineteenth century and the *fin de siècle*.

What is striking, however, is the number of similarities, in terms of both form and content, between those early years of shopping mania and the present late period whose excesses we now see as a symptom of the predicament and decline of traditional retailing. Cultural philosopher Walter Benjamin praised the 'phantasmagoria' of nineteenth-century Paris (the 'capital of luxury and fashion'): 'the enthronement of the merchandise and the splendour of distraction surrounding it'. These are words which can be applied without reservation to today's experience-focused retail design.

At that time the first iron and glass arcades and their successors, the great department stores, were the new emblems of the great cities, equal in status to the central railway station, the opera house or the grand hotel. As late as 1918 no less a figure than Gabriele d'Annunzio was commissioned to come up with a name for a new department store, and his proposal was: La Rinascente. In his era, too, these sumptuous retail oases – whose Parisian prototype was immortalized by Emile Zola in his novel *Au bonheur des Dames* (1883) – stood out against the real-life inhospitability of their urban environment.

What Zola celebrated as 'the modern creation of a dream palace, a babel of storeys towering one on top of another', is once again the prevailing architectural repertoire in postmodern mega-malls and urban shopping centres. The delight in ornamentation and quotation is boundless: majestic rotundas, spectacular air wells, imposing arcades, bold escalator constructions borrow freely from the vocabulary of their historical models and from all stylistic eras.

'Domestizing' the senses From 'privation' to 'desire' is how conservative cultural sociologist Arnold Gehlen once described the path of progressive civilization, which, in Gehlen's view, has to devote ever more ingenuity to producing things that are 'desirable'. Today the psychology of persuasion is calculated in a much more polished and refined way than in the great department stores of the past. In shopping centres, the layout of intermixed store types is arranged to form trails of attraction which meander from the entrance areas through to the main customer magnets, the anchor stores.

What awaits the customers is an interior space protected by CCTV and security staff, eliminating all the disruptions and disturbances of the city jungle outside, fulfilling the demand for urban-style shopping 'reserves', for an undisturbed consumer experience in a stylish setting. At the same time this type of retail format facilitates the conditioning, or 'domestizing' of the senses to what the merchandise promises and money alone can secure. Passers-by are 'domestized' into customers in their experiences and sensations. This conditioning is part of a system 'which makes even strolling exploitable for the purpose of selling merchandise' (Walter Benjamin).

The trend towards homogeneity is increasingly apparent: the spectrum of stores and brands is steadily reducing down to a uniform palette. A trend that initially started in the US malls is now also affecting European and Asian cities: the range of retail and experience products on offer is becoming increasingly standardized. The experience-focused dramatization of the urban experience uses the same props and accessories again and again. Beyond the spectre of the internet economy, it is here, perhaps, that the most fearsome enemy awaits. For the disappearance of differences flattens out the quality of the experience. Honoré de Balzac's effusive enthusiasm – 'The great poem of the shop windows sings out its stanzas of colours from the Madeleine to Porte Saint-Denis' – no longer rings true when the song is the same everywhere. Architecture and the design of retail spaces may have recovered their prestige as marketing tools but they are only really useful when not only the architectural and design wrappings but also the objects of consumer desire deliver what the architectural setting promises, so that the goods themselves are the real experience in the end.

chapter one corporate glamour

Brands on display

The customer is king: that was the formula often cited in the days before e-commerce, but now yesterday's rhetoric has become hard reality. In the new internet economy, markets are transparent and prices are becoming globally comparable. The brand's strength and status are the only things that count in the battle for customers and market share. It is therefore no anachronism that the architectural brand identity conveyed through showrooms, flagship stores and POS designs is currently gaining significance. This deliberate self-dramatization is a core strategic response to the challenges of e-commerce. Distinctive environments are designed to deliver atmospheric experiences which directly benefit the standing of brand and product, while reflecting the necessary changes in distribution patterns. These efforts to kindle and sustain customers' interests are designed to achieve a direct, unmediated commercial relationship between producer and end-consumer – a 'business-to-consumer' strategy that heralds the end of traditional sales channels and intermediaries. These are the common goals shared by an automotive theme park, multimedia outlets and high-class fashion temples: now nothing and nobody stand between the glamour of the brand and the customer's patronage.

opposite: The architects of the Herman Miller Showroom in Chicago created a cool, predominantly white stage set in which the examples of high-quality office furniture could be seen as 'exhibits', removed from their usual environment.

Herman Miller Showroom

Chicago, Illinois, USA, 1998
Interior Design:
Krueck & Sexton Architects

Chicago is the main centre for the US office furniture industry, and this is where the top trade fair, NeoCon, is held. The industry's most prestigious building, the Merchandise Mart is here, too, and so of course Herman Miller, a brand which became famous for its exemplary designs, also has a long-established show-room in the city. Revamping this location was a top-drawer assignment: a brand that achieved global prominence with the legendary collections by George Nelson, Charles and Ray Eames and Bruce Burdick was duty-bound to set contemporary standards for product presentation. The company, which was founded in Michigan in 1923, is now one of the leading office furniture manufacturers in the United States, with a workforce of 8,000 and a turnover of US $ 1.8 billion – and it still operates according to a clear philosophy: 'We value design because it is the way we serve our customers better than anyone else. We start with the real world, with real people, and with real problems. Design is about solving those real world problems. Always seeking to improve and, at its best, surprise, design enables us to leap to radically new places with entirely new solutions. Design can and should be reflected in all that we do. Great design leads to new insight, understanding, and innovation.'

Krueck & Sexton Architects were engaged to overhaul the Chicago showroom, and from the outset they dispensed with any analogy to real office environments, designing instead a minimalist stage set to present changing exhibits. The items of furniture are displayed individually, with the accent on their status as objects. The long, jagged glass front which extends from the entrance through to the reception area,

above: Items of furniture on display are given object status by placing them in minimalist surroundings; cool white abounds, from the terrazzo floor to the walls, ceilings and surfaces.

opposite: A long zig-zagging glass passageway runs from the Showroom's entrance to reception area, offering inviting views inside – transparency is the hallmark of the design.

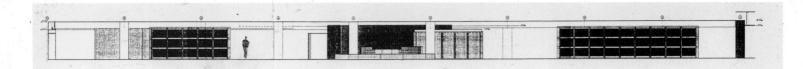

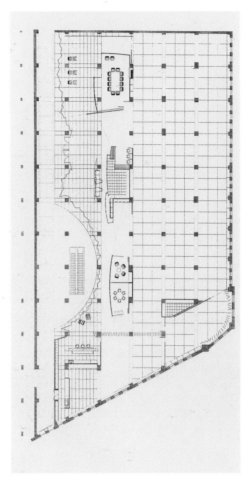

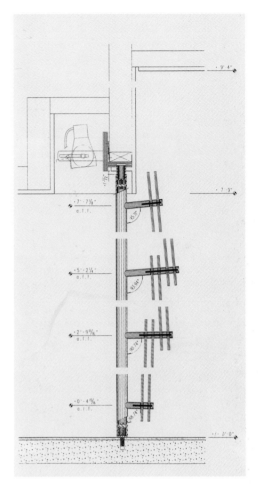

offering extensive views of the interior, is designed to tempt outside observers strolling along the passageway to come inside. Transparency is the leitmotif of this 'eye-catching space that would look great whether full of furniture or completely empty' (Krueck & Sexton). Meeting areas are located behind panes of glass printed with grids of dots, fast-moving back projections are used to dematerialize other wall sections made of sandblasted glass.

All the materials used are white in colour, from the terrazzo of the flooring, and the walls and ceilings, through to the reception counters, but subtle lighting effects create a dynamic spatial effect, preventing any impression of clinical functionality. The colours on the walls are modulated by computer, changing from red, through yellow, blue and green to rich purple. The theatrical, almost cinematic (with the changing light effects) quality of this interior design not only separates the furniture on display from its actual intended function, it also provides an interesting response to the steady erosion of the traditional office environment. In a world where company structures are increasingly devolving into virtual networks and desk-bound employees are becoming free-ranging web surfers, even useful products can turn into the exhibits of an artificially distanced brand gallery.

above left and opposite: Meeting areas are located behind curving screens of louvred glass panels which form a contrast to the straight glass panels of the zig-zagging route.

top: Cross-section

above: Plan

above: Drawing of the support mechanism for the glass panelled screen.

A theatrical use of changing light, controlled by computer, subtly transforms the environment with background hues of pinks and purples, reds and greens; the result is an ambient space a world away from the traditional office.

Giorgio Armani

Paris, France, 1999
Interior Design:
Claudio Silvestrin Architects

It was inevitable that the two would come together: Giorgio Armani, master of classical minimalist fashions, and Claudio Silvestrin, the creator of pared-down interiors, form the perfect duo. Add an address on Paris' prestigious Place Vendôme to a collaboration between the two and you could expect the result to be outstanding. It is.

Armani gave his architect a completely free hand and Silvestrin took the opportunity to create an apotheosis both of his own style – already established via a series of remarkable projects – and of the aura and image of the Armani brand. It is said that a monastery once stood on this site, but even without this historical connection, Silvestrin's austere retail sanctuary, featuring the stoically impressive solidity of unpolished stone and solid ebony, would have become a very special place of pilgrimage in its own right.

With this project Silvestrin took the next logical step along a path he had already mapped out in his early shop designs for other leading fashion names. However, if one compares the Paris store Silvestrin created for Calvin Klein in 1997 with this latest project, the even more abstract, and at the same time more refined character of the spatial and ornamental solutions is striking.

Silvestrin described his goal as being 'To create a space that transcends minimalism and instead strives for the timeless elegance that is the essence of Place Vendôme itself'. This philosophy is already apparent from outside: the listed sandstone façade was restored and carefully sandblasted, only the Armani signature in gold indicates what lies within. The interior begins with the seven-metre-high

above: The listed sandstone façade of the boutique on the prestigious Place Vendôme was meticulously restored.

opposite: Armani gave Silvestrin free reign to exercise his purist sensibilities, creating a 'sanctuary' of unpolished stone surfaces and solid ebony furniture; to carry the analogy further, there is even a stone 'font'.

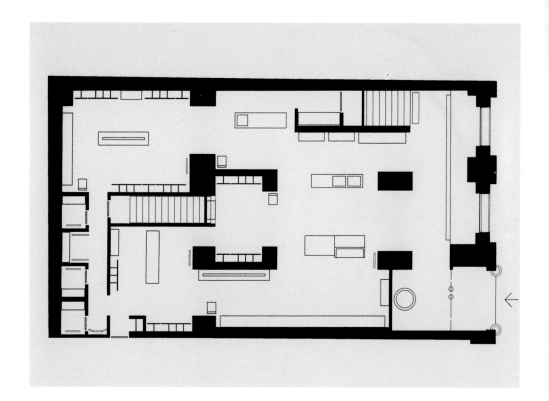

entrance hall, which is entered through a glass front set back from the façade: as a kind of vestibule or antechamber to the fashion temple itself. It even has a font: Silvestrin's trademark circular pool is the only object it contains. From here, customers are led off to one side towards the awe-inspiring realm of the precious merchandise.

The two-storey, 450 square metre space is divided up in a simple, rectangular arrangement. There is nothing to disrupt the elegant proportions of the walls and fittings. The lights are set flush into the ceilings and stone walls, or else they shine indirectly from behind bronze pillars. The high-backed, monumental chairs – almost medieval in appearance – are still immaculate, but this will not last: soon the first cracks will appear in what the company insists is macassar wood sourced from licensed suppliers. This fits with the whole concept: patina, after all, is a vital ingredient of timelessness. The collections may change with each season, but their classical setting is allowed to age gracefully.

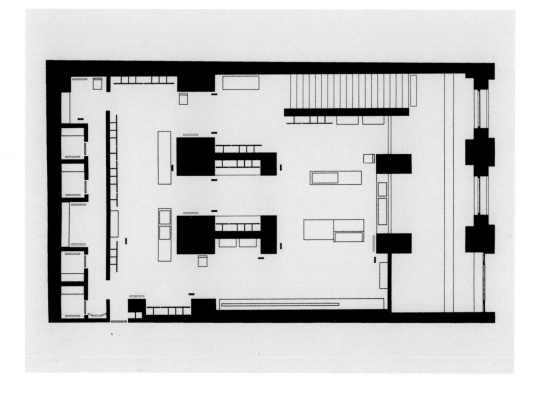

top: Ground floor plan

above: First floor plan

Simple geometrical
volumes are divided
and defined by carefully
positioned furniture in
dark African ebony,
which sets off the paler
tones of walls and floor.

Zumtobel
Staff
Lichtzentrum

Berlin, Germany, 1999
Interior Design:
Sauerbruch Hutton Architekten

The area directly next to the Oberbaumbrücke in Berlin, where, until German reunification, the River Spree formed the border between East and West, is also a historically significant one for the lighting industry. It was here, shortly after 1900, that one of the world's largest lamp factories of its era came into being: the headquarters of the Osram brand. In the 1990s the entire complex – originally designed by Peter Schwechter, the architect of Berlin's Gedächtniskirche – was renovated, preserving the original architectural fabric. The exemplary reclamation of this historic industrial ensemble attracted new occupants including architecture- and design-based companies, planning departments, advertising agencies and publishers. Berlin's International Design Centre has also been based here since 1997. And so there were a number of good reasons for Zumtobel Staff, one of Europe's largest lighting manufacturers, to choose this as the location for its branch in the German capital.

The Berlin-based Sauerbruch Hutton team, leading representatives of the younger generation of Berlin architects who had already achieved recognition for a series of outstanding projects, were commissioned as designers. The striking qualities of their larger projects are also evident in this relatively small design commission, which covers an area of 1,230 square metres. The spatial experience as a perfect synthesis of form, colour and light: this is the distinguishing feature of the new showroom on the ground floor as well as the offices and conference facilities in the upper storeys.

The aim was to create a unique world of lighting effects within the existing façade of the historic building. Sauerbruch Hutton explain:

above: It was appropriate that lighting firm Zumtobel Staff chose to house its Berlin branch in the former Osram lamp factory: the design team aimed to create a unique arena of lighting effects set against the organic forms of partitions and suspended ceilings.

opposite: A glass screen with a poem on light on its surface guides passers-by into the courtyard.

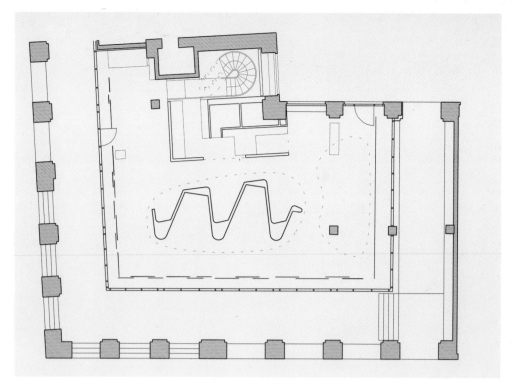

'Natural and artificial light, together with colour
and plasticity, are the themes. Diverse spatial
configurations provide the set for varied lighting
situations, from the daylight ceiling to exhibition
and workplace lighting.' Coloured glass
screens, set inside the actual windows, act as
daylight filters in the showroom, defining backdrops for displaying products and lighting
solutions. On the ground floor, a floating wall
forms a striking space divider, creating niches
to separate the various lighting installations. A
wide spiral staircase, illuminated by a light wall,
leads with a brilliant flourish up to the first floor,
where all the offices and meeting rooms also
present individual lighting solutions. The varied
colour scheme heightens the architectural
impact of the manifold contours on the
ceilings and walls.

For Zumtobel Staff, the collaboration with
Sauerbruch Hutton is one of an ongoing series
of architectural projects undertaken by the
group. Hans Hollein designed the company's
Lichtforum ('Light Forum') in Vienna in 1996,
Julia Bolles-Wilson and Peter Wilson designed
the forum at Lemgo in Westphalia in the same
year. In 1999, the Snøhetta group was commissioned to design the lighting centre in Oslo,
while Jean Michel-Wilmotte was entrusted
with the Paris branch, which opened in
autumn 2000.

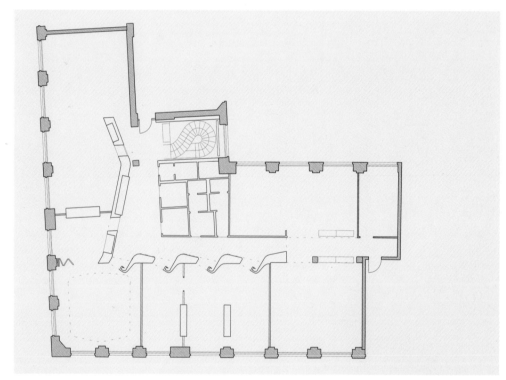

top: Ground floor plan

above: First floor plan

**opposite and top left:
A spiral staircase
illuminated by a
brilliantly coloured
wall sweeps up to the
first-floor offices and
meeting rooms – the
wall heightens the
architectural impact of
the store by contrasting
with the curved
contours of the light
above.**

**opposite and above:
The floating partitions
create diverse spatial
arrangements which
are punctuated by
outdoor light strips
streaming in-between
and through the
coloured screens.**

Nike Town

London, UK, 1999
Interior Design: BDP Design,
Nike Retail Design

War has been raging in the world of sports retailing since the market brand leader decided not to play by the traditional rules of the game. Nike wants to become more independent of what has until now been its most important distribution channel; it is seeking to liberate itself from the monopolistic power of the trade pools and its major customers. To this end the group is significantly reducing the number of authorized outlets and expanding its market presence via its own stores, in-store retail outlets and e-commerce. The strategic goal here is not difficult to guess: if the company no longer allows third parties to come between the brand and its end consumers, then it will have, both on-line and on-site, full control of the entire commercial chain, from production via marketing and distribution through to end sales, and including profit margins.

The company's flagship stores, trading under the Nike Town banner, are battleships in this retail war. They clearly embody the global aspirations of the giant and are designed to exercise an irresistible attraction over the hearts and minds of young, trend-conscious consumers.

The Nike Town on Oxford Circus, which opened in 1999, is even bigger and considerably more spectacular than its New York predecessor of 1996; and it delivers what its name promises, in every respect. A traditional London department store – a listed building – which had long degenerated into a bargain

BDP and Nike devised a city theme for the London home of the brand; a brick-faced 'street' looks on to the Nike pavilion.

basement for dozens of fashion labels, was implanted with a 'hybrid concept of a city' as Nike's Global Creative Director John Hoke proudly declares. The simulated indoor cityscape borrows from legendary sports venues in London as well as picking up on popular, even eccentric details of life in the city. London-based design team BDP Design collaborated with the company's own team of professionals to produce the design. They set their sights high, saying: 'a London home for Nike becomes an ambassador for the brand, provides a new milestone in the Nike Town story and an environment which allows itself to speak specifically to its London and European customers'.

As customers walk through this Swoosh City they are surrounded by the façades of a variety of pavilions, each devoted to a different type of sport; the complex as a whole covers more than 6,500 square metres over three galleried storeys. Metal bridges lead to the central tower construction where the brand's future techno-logical potential is celebrated in an audiovisual electronic display of merchandise. Nor is the sporting past neglected: authentic items of sports gear worn by national and international sporting megastars are displayed in shrines like 'crown jewels', as John Hoke describes them. Whether these flagships – after New York and London, the next Nike Town will be located in Tokyo – will help Nike win its retail battle is as yet unclear, but one thing at least seems certain: anyone who makes the voyage to buy their Nike trainers and sports gear in the home of Nike itself will certainly find all the other places where the brand is simply piled on the shelves distinctly dull by contrast.

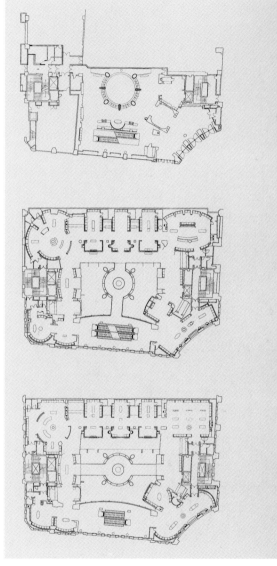

opposite: The escalator
area is connected to
the Nike pavilion by
metal deck bridges.

above: The colourfully
lit central Nike pavilion,
celebrating the sports
company's technologi-
cal developments and
potential in audio-visual
displays, forms the
heart of the store and
acts as an electronic
'town crier'.

above: Ground floor
plan (top), first floor
plan (centre) and sec-
ond floor plan (bottom).

Superga

Madrid, Spain, 1998
Interior Design: Studio Iosa Ghini

Since 1911, rubber has been the focus of everything for Turin-based company Superga. The brand achieved international renown for a number of products, but principally for its canvas shoes with non-slip soles which first appeared on the market in 1925. All that it needed to give it the decisive push into cult status was the requisite retail ambience, and in 1996 none other than Massimo Iosa Ghini was engaged for this purpose. This trained architect and successful designer had made a name for himself with unusual showroom and point-of-sale projects for such diverse customers as Ferrari, Maserati, Fiorucci, Omnitel and Infostrada.

The starting point for his designs is the socio-critical observation by American academic Jeremy Rifkin that 'we are heading towards a future where products are increasing and consumers decreasing'. From which Iosa Ghini in turn draws the wise conclusion that 'we will spend our money and time in places that lend meaning to our existence'. If we follow this observation then in the case of Superga, too, the key issue is not so much selling products as conveying a brand message: 'This leads us to set the term "store" aside and to think more and more in terms of "mediologic gallery", where you do not just go and buy a quality product, but you also purchase the quality culture that generated it'. And entirely in the spirit of Marshall McLuhan, Iosa Ghini defines the key material, rubber, as Superga's primary medium for communicating with its customers, on an aesthetic and emotional level. Rubber is omnipresent in the store concept, which can be applied both as a modular display system

The brand itself was the inspiration for Iosa Ghini's all-rubber modular design system for Superga: shelving made of glass coated with rubber and lit from behind provides a translucent backdrop to the shoes hung from rotating metal holders.

A striking mur
Ghini forms a
backdrop to th
lar system of c
units and furn
within the stor

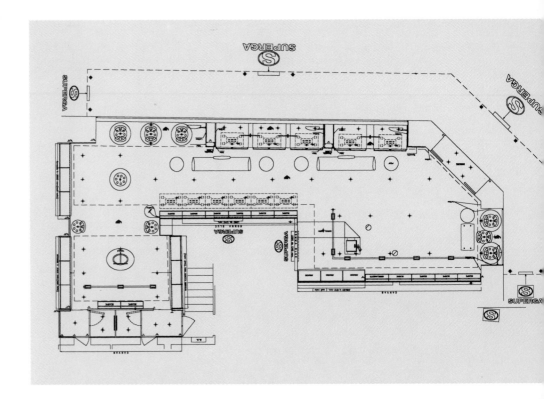

or as a complete interior. Rubber on the walls
and translucent shelves, rubber-coated fabrics
for the seating, rubber in the form of latex
paints used for all the fittings, even rubber in
liquid form in the upholstery.

Larger-scale Superga stores following this
format were initially set up in Italian cities.
International expansion soon followed, and
with each new project Iosa Ghini perfected the
design even further. The Madrid branch, which
opened in 1998, can lay claim to be the best
yet. It is set in an old building, a property
whose commercial past is signalled by ornate
iron pillars and vaulted ceilings. The modular
Superga world was deliberately set into the
existing structure in the manner of a temporary
installation – yet the overall impression is
entirely convincing.

top: Plan

**above: Even the
brightly coloured
furnishings continue
the theme with liquid
rubber upholstery.**

Stylish, organically
shaped display
columns with inset
lighting systems
indicate the level of
sophistication achieved
with the modular
system in Madrid, the
latest in a series of
similar Superga
projects by Iosa Ghini.

Levi's Flagship Store

Regent Street, London, UK, 1999
Interior Design:
Checkland Kindleysides

Old age comes to all of us eventually – even to cult brands like Levi's. The classic jeans manufacturer relied too long on yesterday's myths and learned this painful lesson to its cost when its sales figures collapsed in the late 1990s. The youth of today's international street culture are not remotely attracted by Western-style fashions or 1950s nostalgia: in the eyes of Generation X, the standard leisurewear sported by their parents is seriously uncool. Once the market strategists of the Dino company – founded by the Levi family nearly a century and a half ago – had grasped this fact they put all their marketing energies into changing course. The about-turn was given its most radical expression in the new design for the Levi's Flagship Stores.

First in the company's home town of San Francisco, and then in London's West End, British interior designers Checkland Kindleysides were entrusted with inventing multimedia/interactive brand theme parks: the goal was to 'create an environment where fashion, art and music converge', said Janie Ligon, Levi's Vice-President DTC. Checkland Kindleysides designed the Regent Street flagship store, completed in the autumn of 1999, as a 'totally flexible space' on two storeys and over 930 square metres, which with 'movable screens and walls' conveys the 'impression of a large exhibition area' in order 'to create a retail experience as opposed to a retail environment'. The impressive DJ-Tower, a two-storey cylinder in which the duty soundmaster produces rave-mixes from behind a perforated steel screen, provides a link between the ground floor and the basement – accompanied, of course, by the obligatory chill-out

above: The store is designed as an entirely flexible space which can be reconfigured with changing needs; today's demanding 15-24 year olds are encouraged to customize their Levi's into personal works of art in a special area in the basement.

opposite: Music is pumped out from the resident DJ's cylindrical sounds tower which rises up from the basement to the ground floor. A stainless steel and glass bridge dissects the stairwell revealing views to the lower level.

zone. The other props in this multimedia production include video projections, computer terminals with internet access, temporary art installations and record and book counters.

To ensure that this acoustic/visual overkill does not obscure the real commercial purpose of the experience, walk-in boxes have been installed which use digital body screening techniques to supply garment measurements for a perfect fit, and in the Customization Area in the basement customers can turn their Levi's – newly purchased or brought from home – into one-off works of art using laser etchings, embroidery or special dyes. This retail environment is deliberately focused on entertainment, which surrounds – even obscures – the presentation of the merchandise. Yet this does not necessarily mean that the client and the designers have missed the mark: their goal is to keep their target group, aged between 15 and 24, within the Levi's theme park for as long as they can, until its attractions are transferred to the fashions on offer and the frenzy of music and images finally gives way to the ringing of the cash till.

Comfortable low seating is provided beneath the stairs – chill-out zones are combined with video projections and computer terminals with internet access to entertain customers while they shop.

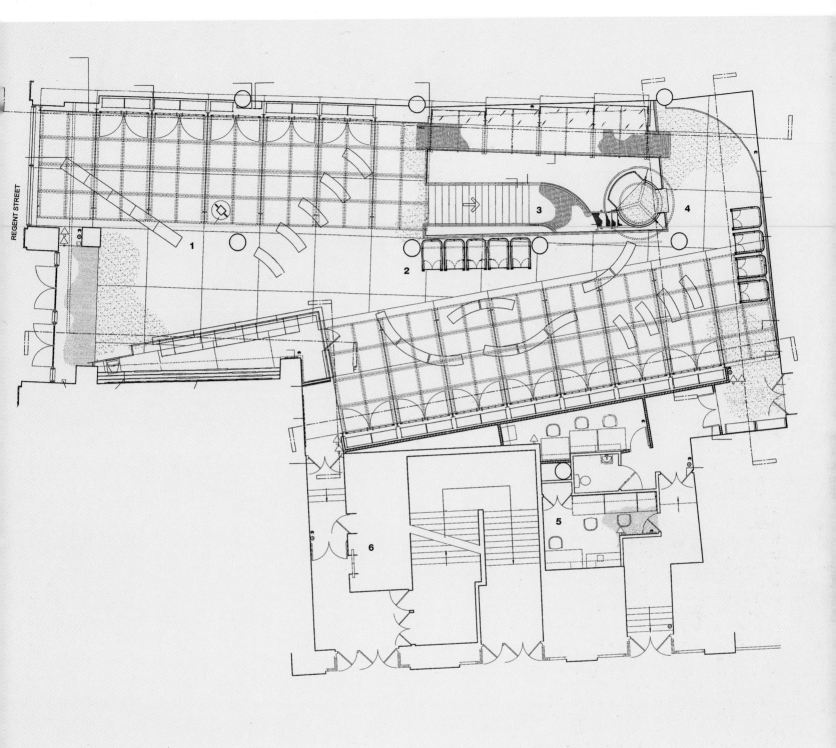

REGENT STREET

Ground floor plan
1 low display tables
2 mobile changing
  rooms
3 stairs
4 DJ tower
5 office
6 lift

Moschino

London, UK, 1998
Interior Design: Hosker Moore & Kent

How can a fashion brand based on provocative, light-hearted chic be kept alive when the creative force behind it is no more? Franco Moschino died in 1994, certainly not in such dramatic fashion as his more famous compatriot and fellow designer Gianni Versace, but his death too was no small shock for the fashion world. Many in the industry predicted the demise of his collections, which had become notorious for their irony, wit and up-front meanings. There was little else left for the surviving management to do but make the lost master's creations into a classic paradigm with a high recognition value. Logically, it was decided that the future corporate image of the stores and in-store outlets needed a retail concept which reflected the spirit of the designer. This in turn meant that the minimalistically-inclined interior designers Hosker Moore & Kent were forced to overcome their own internal barriers: 'We had to try and distil the essence of Moschino and do things the way he would have done. We were going to have to break all the design codes we had been brought up with. It was very difficult trying to discern all the positive elements and those that we could take forward. We wanted some chaos but with control,' said Peter Kent.

Since 1996 the London-based team has been working on the new Moschino universe, based on a standard vocabulary of symbols,

The world's largest Moschino store in London mutates the anarchic, symbolic elements of the late designer's work into new refinement and elegance.

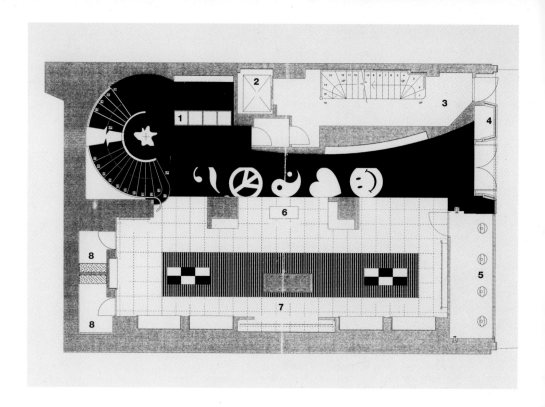

patterns, shapes and colours. Each of the five product lines – the top-price label Moschino Couture!, the more accessible Cheap & Chic range, the accessories business Moschino Borse, Moschino Jeans and Moschino Men – were given their own distinct identity within the overall stylistic concept. Like a box of chocolates, these identities can be positioned individually – over the different areas of a top department store, for example – or brought together for maximum impact in a flagship store.

The latter is the case in Conduit Street in London's West End, where one of the world's largest Moschino stores was opened in 1998. Here, the interiors of two existing buildings were completely redesigned. All the collections are displayed over 790 square metres on the ground and first floors, while the three storeys above this house the showrooms and offices of Moschino's UK head office. 'Pop baroque' is the term Peter Kent uses for the creation he has brilliantly extrapolated from Franco Moschino's kaleidoscope of kitsch: 'We've exploited many of the key elements in the process of creating a clear image which accurately reflects the message of each collection. We have clarified rather than recreated the Moschino image.' The anarchic fun of the past is still in evidence, but it is presented in such an elegant, refined way that it has the quality of a distant memory. The order of things has been inverted: once the mischievous Moschino raided the treasure trove of everyday myths and symbols; now hearts, peace-signs and the like have become the brand souvenirs of a deceased fashion rebel.

top: Ground floor plan
1 cash desk
2 lift
3 offices entrance
4 display window
5 main display window
6 display table
7 chaise longue
8 changing room

above: Elevation of ground and first floors, showing some of the visual puns of the design.

opposite: A pathway to the 'Pop baroque' golden staircase is laid out with an eclectic collection of graphic symbols which reflect the Moschino image.

opposite: Hosker
Moore & Kent designed
theatrical settings for
the different ranges of
clothes, clarifying the
different product lines
on offer.

above: A gloriously
kitsch window display
(lined with *Financial
Times* newspaper) is
both self- and location-
referential; the spirit of
fun pays homage to the
designer.

Swatch
Timeship

New York, New York, USA, 1996
Interior Design: Pentagram Design

Times change. For many years Chanel occupied three storeys on 57th Street between Fifth and Madison Avenues – then Parisian haute couture gave way to the low-tech of Swiss plastic watches. The Swatch Timeship, a stylish, futuristic hybrid of showroom and strongroom covering just under 470 square metres, opened in late 1996, with perfect timing for the rush of Christmas trading.

The team from Pentagram Design was led by Daniel Weil from London, who was thoroughly familiar with the Swatch brand. He had collaborated as a consultant on the packaging concept for the Irony range of watches, and as a prominent representative of 1980s British design he was entirely familiar with the marketing concept and leading designers behind the Swatch success story – based on elevating budget products to the status of cult objects by means of avant-garde ornamentation.

Weil's motto was: 'Like a Swatch watch, the store is "machinery with personality"'. Behind the glass façade, a colossal 'Jelly' model, two storeys high, signals the kingdom of plastic timekeepers. On the ground floor is an elongated sales area, bordering at the far end on the Club Chamber, a treasure trove of collectors' items: resplendent on the Collector's Wall are row upon row of classic models which sold out years ago and are now traded for high prices. Visitors who go up to Dr. Swatch's spare parts store in the mezzanine are surrounded by the hissing of Swatch watches being pneumatically propelled through transparent tubes. This traditional dispatch system, used in other commercial contexts to transport paperwork and cash, is transformed in the Timeship into a futuristic capillary network connecting the stockroom

above: The glazed façade is framed with blue textured stainless steel, creating three panels. The giant 'Jelly' watch has become a landmark timepiece for the busy shoppers on 57th Street.

opposite: Reflective surfaces reinforce a sense of movement and encourage the visitor's eye to settle on the watches. The gaps between the staircase treads act as a projection surface allowing illuminated, animated images of Swatch inspirations to be visible from the street.

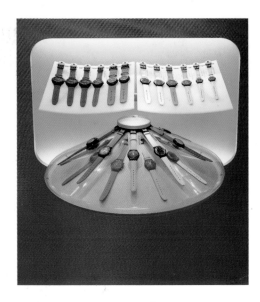

and the sales counters. On the top floor is the Swatch Gallery: a museum-style display of artists' editions – watch designs by Keith Haring, Annie Leibowitz, Yoko Ono and other famous names. Screens throughout the Timeship bombard visitors and customers with a constant stream of images: classic ad campaigns alternate with reports on events connected with the brand.

When the Manhattan flagship opened, the brand was urgently in need of an image makeover; the trendsetting company was increasingly concerned about competition from younger labels trading on nostalgia rather than imaginatively embellished plastic. Business picked up again – but this was not so much due to new retail concepts as to new product features and formats. With perfect timing for the new millennium, Swatch was able to announce record sales figures. And the moral of this story is: image and ambience are not everything, for cult products in particular it is not just a question of up-to-the-minute presentation – both the message and the contents must also keep pace with the times.

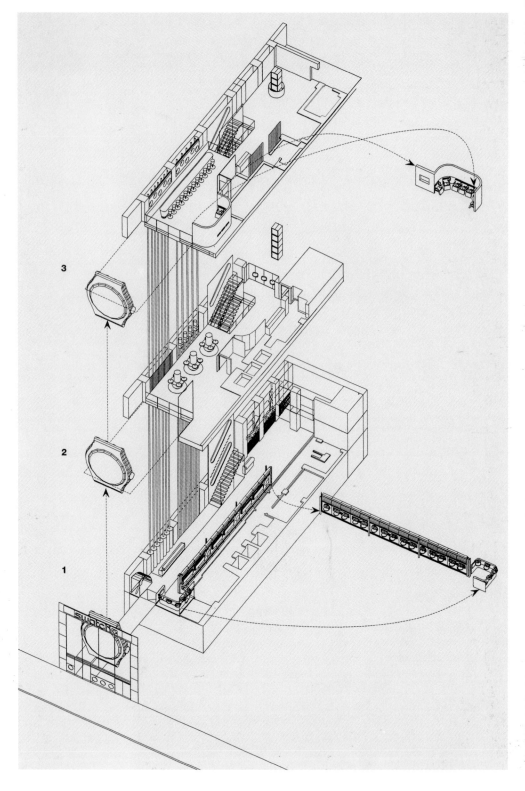

top left: Rows of past and present watches are displayed in museum style along a Collector's Wall located in the double height Club Chamber.

above: Exploded axonometric
1 ground floor
2 first floor
3 second floor

Swatches are pneumatically propelled throughout the store via a capillary network of transparent tubes, in an adaptation of the traditional shop cash dispatch system; the background hiss makes the Timeship come alive with sound.

Pakhuis

Amsterdam, The Netherlands, 1999
Architecture / Interior Design:
Meyer en van Schooten Architecten

The need for historic port has dwindled with today's standardized container freight – this applies just as much in Amsterdam as it does in London's Docklands or on the piers of Barcelona. So, programmes of demolition and conversion are underway in these abandoned wastelands, transforming them into new city districts. On Amsterdam's former main quay, the empty storehouses stand in rows, most of them displaying in large, faded characters the names of the lands from where goods were once imported.

Since early 1999 the huge, five-storey brick building once called 'Asia' has been known simply as the 'Pakhuis', yet instead of stacks of goods the building now houses elegantly arranged luxury collections by internationally renowned interior design firms, spread over a total of 7,630 square metres on all floors. More than 30 manufacturers of furniture, fabrics, lighting and accessories have taken possession of this rejuvenated space, using it as a shared showroom for their own displays. Nothing is actually sold here, but members of the public are welcome to visit alongside the trade clientele – the idea is that they get information here and then order the items of their choice from appointed dealers located throughout The Netherlands. Within a very short period this commercial concept has proved a tremendous success, and the Pakhuis has become a place of pilgrimage for the growing community of design afficionados.

This pulling power is in large part due to the distinctive style of Roberto E. Meyer and Jeroen W. van Schooten, the local architects responsible for the conversion. Their design was defined by three criteria: 'Respecting the

above: The designer furniture showrooms that have set up home in the former 'Asia' warehouse enjoy views on to the old port area of Amsterdam – and across to contemporary urban development.

opposite: The interior shows how Meyer and van Schooten respected the original fabric of the building, only intervening with minimalist care: new staircases cut through old ceilings allowing much more light to infiltrate the space.

existing building and the structure of it with the
new elements added opposite the existing
elements as much as possible; using minimalist materials in order to create contrasts with
critical care; creating a clear routing through
the building.' To brighten up the gloomy
mezzanines, the designers cut large lengthways openings into the ceilings, which now
have new staircases leading through them
from entrance level right up to the top floor.
Separate areas for special uses were set at
either end of the long warehouse space:
offices, conference rooms and, on the second
floor, a lavishly proportioned restaurant with
sundeck. However, anyone enjoying the view
of the water after touring the collections has to
do without a romantic harbour scene to
contemplate: on the opposite bank the urban
future has begun, with rows of brand new
apartment blocks stretching out to the horizon.

**above left: The bright
open spaces freed
up by the renovation
project allowed room
for over 30 design
firms to take up resi-
dence in the building
and showcase their
wares – items are not
actually purchased
here but members
of the public are
welcome.**

**above: Glass staircases
rise from the ground
floor, through the old
timber ceilings, up to
the top floor.**

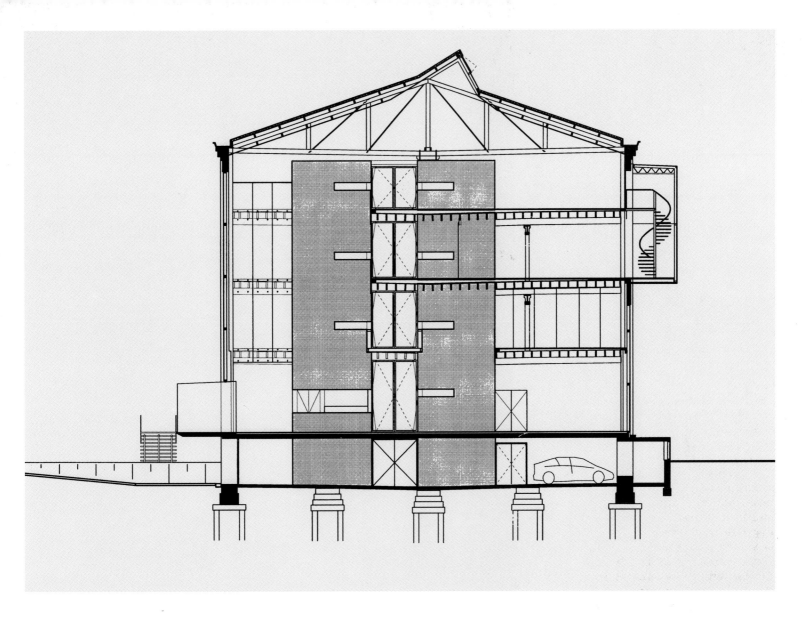

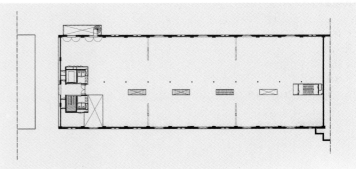

**top: Cross section
showing the five
storeys of the building.**

above: Floor plan

Autostadt

Wolfsburg, Germany, 2000
Architecture: Henn Architekten

Wolfsburg was an 'Autostadt' (car city) from the very beginning – the sole purpose of the new community created in 1938 was to be the home for what was at the time the world's most advanced automotive factory. At the outset military vehicles rolled off the production line rather than the cars – dubbed 'Volkswagen', or people's car – which had been designed by the brilliant engineer Ferdinand Porsche. This reflected the priorities of the real power behind the project: Adolf Hitler had promised the Germans 'Kraft durch Freude' ('power through joy') and millions of VW Beetles, but a World War and campaigns of destruction called for a very different sort of machinery. Wolfsburg and the VW-plant survived the allied bombing with some damage, became the very epitome of the West German economic revival and are now the home of one of the global players in the automotive sector.

Since Ferdinand Piech, grandson of Porsche, has been at the head of the group, the drive towards global leadership in volume terms is no longer the company's primary goal. The plan is to develop Volkswagen – previously, with Audi, synonymous with top quality in the mid-market segment – as an upmarket international umbrella brand. Following acquisitions in the South (Seat) and East (Skoda), the group set its sights rather higher: Rolls Royce, Bentley and Lamborghini. And this top-drawer group, with its mixed bag of a portfolio, needed a top-quality showcase to match – Autostadt was born, the first car theme park, covering a 25-hectare site directly next to the VW plant, with its own Intercity railway station.

The VW-Group invested more than EUR 420 million, synchronized the timing of the project to

above and opposite: Cars awaiting collection at Autostadt are stacked high in two 42-metre glazed towers; the cars are raised to and lowered from their positions by central giant 'fork-lift' poles positioned in the centre of the towers.

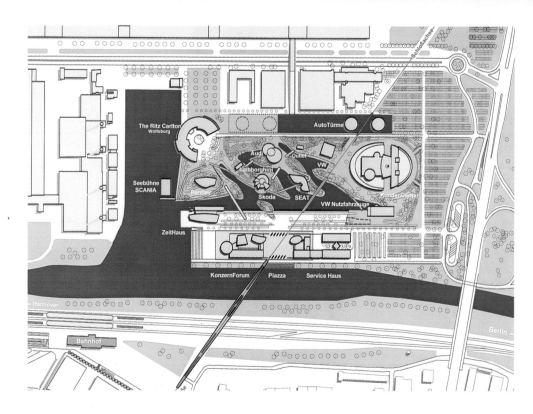

coincide with the EXPO 2000 World Exposition in Hanover, and can rest assured that the pulling-power of this attraction will outlive the international show. 'Visitors can undertake a fascinating journey of discovery into the world of the automobile … they can find out about the plans and visions of one of the world's most important vehicle manufacturers and share in the latest developments … at first hand,' intones the official VW statement. This sort of activity used to be called 'Collection from Works', when purchasers could take delivery of their new vehicle at the plant itself. In Autostadt the vehicles await collection in 42-metre-high glazed tower units. All around this, and preferably on a long visit, customers can immerse themselves in a world of infotainment: each of the group's brands has its own pavilion, and there are technology displays in the KonzernForum and AutoLab, classic cars and a history of transport in the AutoMuseum, a piazza with catering facilities and an obligatory shopping mall.

Munich-based Henn, VW's regular architects, helped themselves liberally to a mixture of styles from contemporary avant-garde architecture: a touch of deconstructivism, a bit of Nouvel, some Herzog & de Meuron, plus a helping of architectural whipped cream in the style of Frank Stella. Sadly, for all the undoubted effort which went into upgrading a brand showcase into an amusement park, the quality of the architecture is proportionately and unremittingly mediocre. It is fortunate that at least the operators of Autostadt's Ritz-Carlton hotel insisted on an internationally presentable designer, engaging Andrée Putman. And so, should Bentley purchasers find themselves in Wolfsburg, at least they can find a decent place to stay the night.

top: Plan of the whole complex showing the location of the various pavilions and entertainment buildings.

above centre: The Volkswagen Pavilion with the car collection towers behind.

above: The Audi Pavilion in its landscaped setting.

above centre: Exterior of the Ritz-Carlton Hotel.

abcove: Entrance to the KonzernForum.

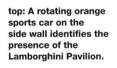

top: A rotating orange sports car on the side wall identifies the presence of the Lamborghini Pavilion.

above: A bridge walkway leads to the Seat Pavilion.

top: The Bentley Pavilion with the chimney stacks of the original Autostadt buildings behind.

above: Entrance to the domed Skoda Pavilion.

opposite: Classic
models such as the VW
Beetle and the Mini on
display in the museum.

above: Huge glazed
doors open up the
façade of the
KonzernForum.

chapter two cool spaces

Retail settings from the gallery to the theatre
Presenting products as so many artefacts and marketing them as original creations has been a tried and trusted formula in fashion and interior design since the late 1980s, or even earlier. For obvious reasons, designers turned to the art world for a retail concept to match. Since then, boutiques and shops have presented themselves as galleries, venues of elegant emptiness and supercool minimalism. But it did not end there. Recently the analogy has been taken further still: designers have consciously reached for museum-style stereotypes, shutting everyday items in glass cases and furnishing sales areas

with display cases just like the ones we have all seen in historical or anthropological collections. In other store designs, the trendspotters themselves are no longer restricted to the role of the admiring onlooker. The customer becomes an actor in the scene, the retail context becomes both catwalk and theme trail. The theatrical element is clear in projects where the route followed by visitors is designed as a mini-drama full of surprises, where the favoured iconography of the relevant customer group is presented in the form of a retail stage-set, or where the same set is used for a succession of changing displays. Even the traditionalists can benefit from this new era in retail

design. For all today's media this is illustrated by the book retailers' return to the unique selling point of their product: light, well-designed club-style facilities await customers for whom reading is still a much-loved leisure pursuit.

opposite: The Win a Cow Free fashion and accessories outlet in Tokyo, Japan, parodies Damien Hirst's famous installations of carcasses in glass showcases to create the ultimate 'cool space'.

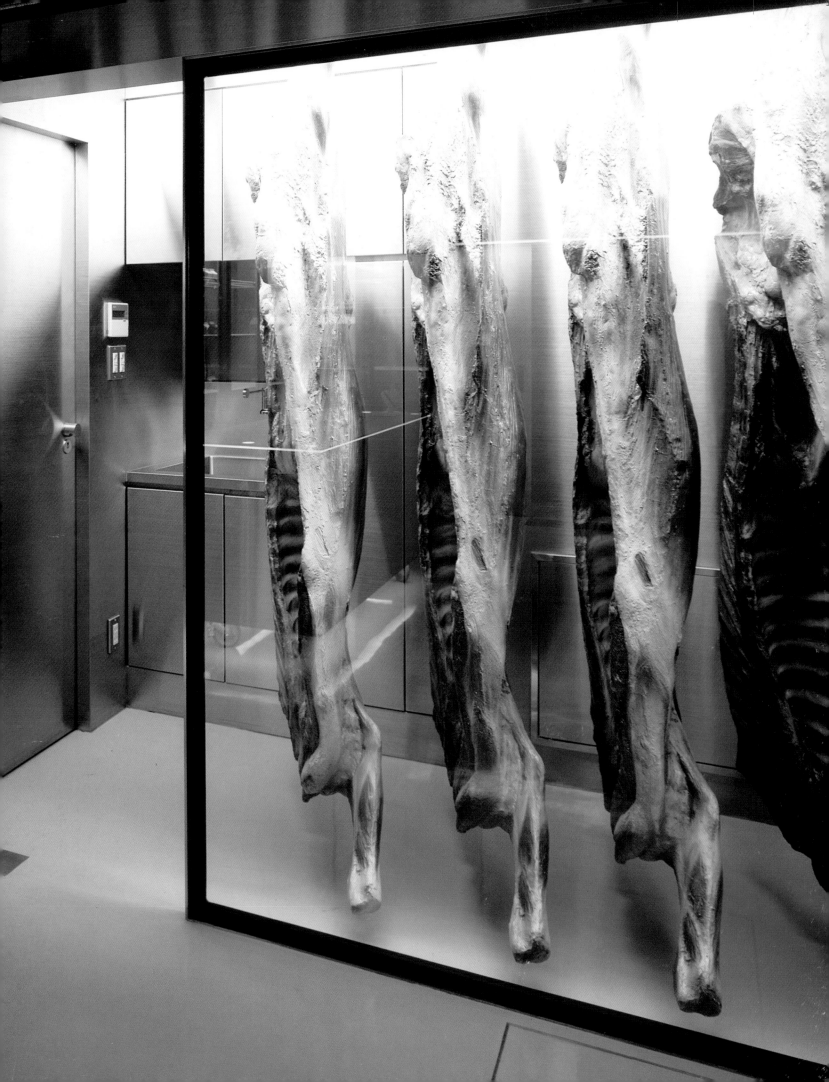

Win a Cow Free

Tokyo, Japan, 1999
Interior Design: Setsumasa Kobashi

Damien Hirst brought the cow into the art gallery. The celebrity artist's neatly carved cadavers in their formalin-filled showcases have become something of an artistic cliché. So it was inevitable that the idea would be copied, even parodied, in less elitist contexts, and the tongue-in-cheek adaptation presented by the fashionable Japanese retailer Setsumasa Kobashi in his cult 'Win a Cow Free' 'message' store in Tokyo has a good deal going for it.

Just as Hirst took the idea of his installations from collections of medical exhibits, so this clinical-looking retail outlet borrows from the repertoire of butchers and supermarkets. The highly perishable merchandise hangs alongside photographs of skinned carcasses as if in refrigerated displays. The products on offer alternate between fashion, accessories, design objects and games, packaged as far as possible in milk cartons and similar mass-market receptacles: 'You can call it a message shop, but you don't sell such a thing as a message. Therefore, we sell products as media and print messages on them. It is accepted that I will print on various items, but I still need to decide what type of items I'd like to sell,' says Kobashi. Each month new themes and product types are selected.

The space was constructed using clinical objects such as a movable counter and glazed display cabinets, utilizing materials which can be washed down like a meat store: stainless steel, aluminium and glass.

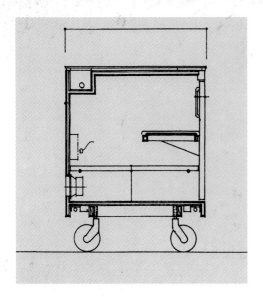

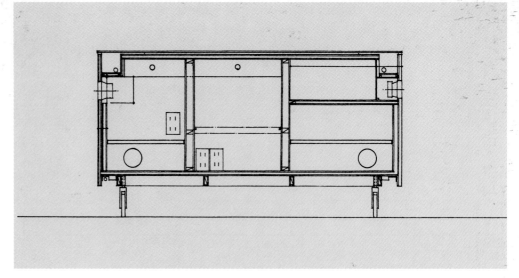

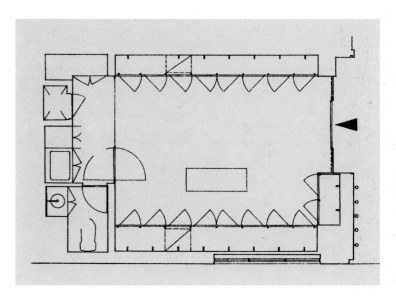

The retail environment is designed for maximum neutrality. Cold light from fluorescent tubes, stainless steel and smooth stone floors, the shop counter as a metal container on wheels: nothing here is remotely homely in feel, for, according to Kobashi, only in an environment that guarantees absolute freshness can his products deliver their bilingual – Japanese or English – message to customers in optimum condition.

However, the name of this cold-storage boutique has nothing to do with Damien Hirst's dead cow obsession: Kobayashi found the slogan 'Win a cow free' by chance in a Las Vegas casino where it was the decorative headline above a row of gaming machines.

above left and top: Detailed drawings of the precisely designed shop counter, which is a metal container on wheels allowing maximum mobility and storage space in an uncluttered environment.

above: Plan of the retail space

The faç
interior's
stainless
Cold fluor
emanating
cabinets
the ceiling
off the sm
coated flo
surfaces i
rule out a
homelines

Rüsing und Rüsing

Düsseldorf, Germany, 2000
Interior Design: Torsten Neeland

Three top-class retail centres specializing in interior design were opened in different German cities in quick succession, trading under the 'Stilwerk' banner. Following after Hamburg (1996) and Berlin (1999), the Düsseldorf branch opened in February 2000, set in a boldly transformed former swimming pool from the 1950s: five storeys, with 17,500 square metres and 45 stores.

The idea behind these centres is that the competition is good for business, but for the individual retailer it is just as important that they present a distinctive design image, ensuring that they make a strong impression among all the other purveyors of beautiful things. Office furnishings supplier Rüsing und Rüsing took the most logical step to achieve this goal and engaged London-based designer Torsten Neeland, originally from Hamburg, who created a sculpted landscape of light and space over 310 square metres. He said: 'My aim was to create an interior design, using light and spatial volume, that would arouse curiosity and create excitement. The space accentuates. Light is consciously used as a medium and comes to the fore.'

Visitors entering the store, on the narrow side of the crooked floorplan, are given a choice: two wall sections, set lengthways on, present them with three alternative routes. On the left, a passageway – 20 metres long and just 1.5 metres wide – is used for the presentation of lights and lighting systems; in the middle is the furniture display area, set behind two light cubes whose colours and brightness

Furniture on isolated display is set in show-case-like wall sections.

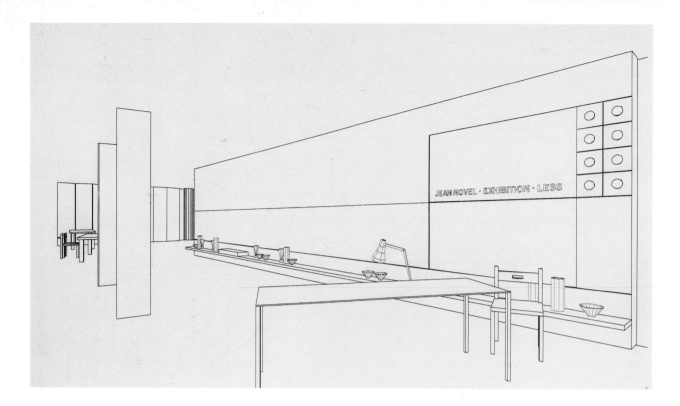

modulate in a steady rhythm; and accessories
are displayed in the area on the right-hand
side. Isolation as a principle of presentation –
display spaces for objects are cut into the wide
wall sections, like showcases – contrasts with
the simulated office spaces at the far end of
the sales area. Here there are variations on the
themes of conference room and workplace
design, along with a kitchen area. Daylight is
filtered through sliding ceiling sections made
of polypropylene.

Neeland himself worked successfully as a
product designer for companies such as
Authentics, Ansorg and Rosenthal and has
produced interior designs for fashion companies and advertising agencies; his work has
long been concerned with the dematerialization
of volumes using light effects. Borrowings from
the art world, and in particular from the light
installations of American artist James Turrell,
are unmistakable. Floating spatial impressions
created by diffuse indirect light, fields of light
set flush with the ceiling, and vertical slits of
light in walls or installation produce Neeland's
tried and trusted repertoire of effects, which
he has re-created in the Düsseldorf Stilwerk
with practised virtuosity. These effects counter-
balance the 'object' character of the furniture
and accessories, blurring the distinction between gallery and showroom – which is entirely
in tune with the concept of up-market office
furnishings. For what the designers of Rüsing
und Rüsing promise their customers is more
than just a functional working environment:
each individual office environment is designed
to express the position, status, style and
personality of the user.

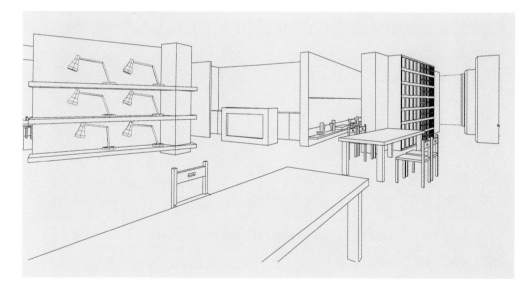

top and above:
Perspective drawings
of the display
configurations.

opposite: Torsten
Neeland – a master of
dematerialized lighting
effects – made best
use of light and space
on an awkward floor-
plan: the customer is
directed down a narrow
passageway which is
successfully utilized
for the display of lamps.

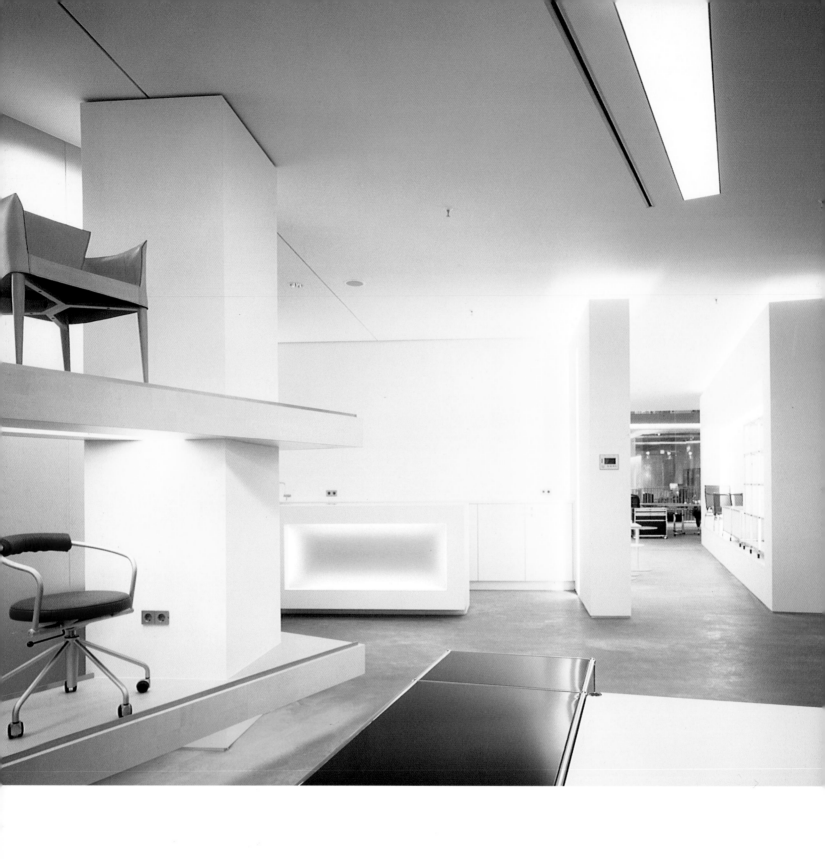

opposite: Furniture is exhibited behind installation-like light cubes in the central section of the shop, and diffuse light emanates from the ceiling and slits in walls – the resulting space is as much gallery as showroom.

above: The Rüsing und Rüsing store itself is located within a successfully transformed swimming pool; Neeland's elegant designs for simulated office spaces are visible through the glass walls.

Advanced Cique

Tokyo, Japan, 1997
Interior Design: Hideo Yasui

For a long time, the prevailing fashion was to present upmarket merchandise in splendid isolation, like diamond solitaires, giving fashion boutiques pretensions to art-gallery status. Turning the interested observer into an uncritical admirer was no bad marketing strategy; individual taste was eclipsed by the dazzle factor of the brand. Yet, in the long run, an excess of cultivated emptiness becomes tedious: a high-class wasteland. It was for this reason that Japanese interior and lighting designer Hideo Yasui quite deliberately reversed the priorities, focusing on the retail experience itself in his award-winning shop designs, which turn the spotlight primarily on the customer rather than exclusively on the merchandise.

The largest and most successful example of Yasui's art of elegantly-lit sales outlets is the fashion boutique Advanced Cique in Tokyo's Aoyama district, an area which has in recent years become a magnet for young, affluent consumers. Over an area of 330 square metres, Yasui created a theatrical landscape whose effectiveness is the product of an enchanting architecture of light; he has said, 'We consider designing with intangible light and using light for performances to be the two most important factors in space design. We do not view light as a functional tool, rather it is a design factor that is just as valuable as form

View of the main entrance façade at night. Hideo Yasui's enchanting lighting scheme presents a tantalizing well of light within to the passer-by.

and material.' In the case of Advanced Cique the entire space is transformed into a light source.

As visitors enter they are surrounded by brightness – indirectly projected, and cleverly diffused; they walk on under-lit steps and platforms, which appear to be suspended, weightlessly, in the air. This grandiose atmospheric effect is achieved through two captivatingly simple strokes of genius: firstly, not a single light source is visible; secondly, t he translucent polycarbonate panelling which is used to structure the space disseminates and reflects the light across the walls and curved ceilings in the subtlest manner. The height of the space, 4.5 metres, was ideal to accommodate both an interestingly shaped ceiling and the additional upper gallery on one side, which is held up by diagonally protruding supports. White surfaces, shimmering metal boxes and sheet metal flooring, combined with glass fittings, underpin the dematerializing effect of the whole.

The customers are in the spotlight: Yasui's theatre of light creates a platform for their own personal vanities. Fashion once again becomes what it really should be: a coveted, ego-boosting accessory. It hardly needs saying that Advanced Cique only stocks leading brands; however, the fact that Yasui's design has been adapted as a formula for a chain of upmarket fashion stores is worthy of note. His shift of focus – from celebrating top-class items to glorifying the customer's experience – seems to pay off commercially, too.

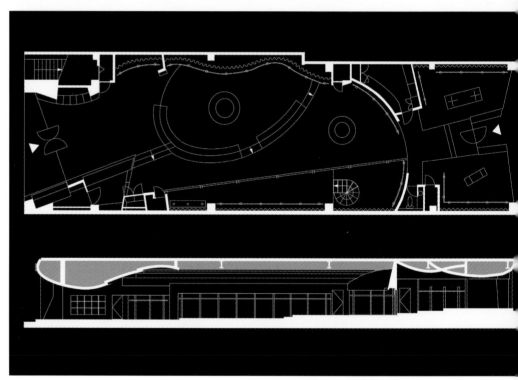

top: The back entrance to the boutique: the customer is guided in past the minimalist glass window displays by lighting at ground level.

above: Plan and section

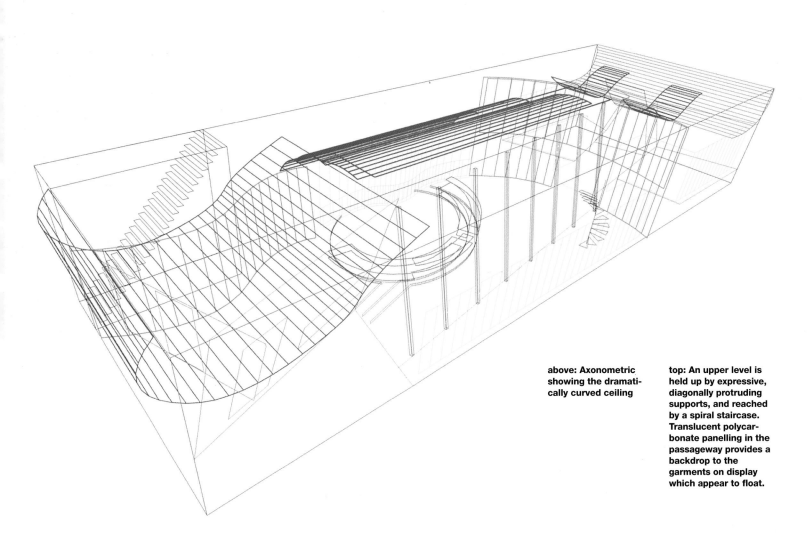

above: Axonometric showing the dramatically curved ceiling

top: An upper level is held up by expressive, diagonally protruding supports, and reached by a spiral staircase. Translucent polycarbonate panelling in the passageway provides a backdrop to the garments on display which appear to float.

The view of the interior from the cashier's point reveals a highly atmospheric architectural arena of airy space and diffused light. Light sources are hidden and under-lit steps and platforms appear to be suspended weightlessly. Customers feel like actors on a stage within the dematerialized setting.

Arsenal

Moscow, Russia, 1997
Interior Design: Natalia Sidorova,
Lorenz Daniil / ABD Company

Whatever the images conjured up by the idea of a Moscow-based arms dealership, especially given the close relationship of business, politics and organized crime in the new Russia, they would certainly have nothing in common with the pared-down, minimalist design of this retail interior. The 'Arsenal', designed by the successful ABD Company, takes the world of weaponry with its sombre aura of camouflage and dark greens, and transposes it into a setting with a contemporary, museum-style ambience.

The lethal merchandise is presented like so many artefacts in tall, freestanding glass cases and in showcases on the walls. This hermetic, distancing effect starts outside the building with its windowless façade. Inside, grey wall panels, granite floors and spot lighting help to create a cold, impersonal atmosphere. The physical appearance of the expensive equipment on display is echoed in the colours and materials of the fittings: the framework of the glass cabinets is made of gleaming matt steel, the long sales and presentation counter of two-tone wood.

The two sales spaces and a private room for VIP customers cover a total area of 175 square metres. The project was completed in just three months, at a total cost of US $210,000. For the designers, who are more used to

Guns as artefacts: the lethal merchandise is for sale but presented in minimalist, spot-lit glass cases.

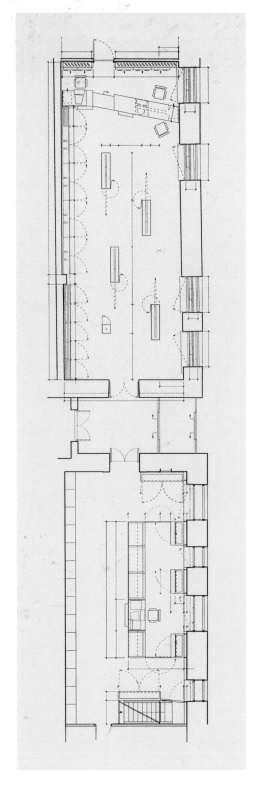

working on civilian projects – interiors for branches of Western banks or car companies, for example – this was a rather unusual assignment. 'The functional meaning of guns is death' – this was the challenge of the project, as laconically summarized by Natalia Sidorova, the young architect responsible for the project. Sidorova found a solution that fulfilled both its aesthetic and functional requirements: what cannot be prettified or glossed over can at least be effectively encased or enshrined. An ingenious mechanism in the cabinets means that any particular item can be swiftly released to the storey below, allowing customers to handle the merchandise and assure them-selves of its quality in private. But such mundanities should not be allowed to spoil the immaculate external appearance of this upmarket gun gallery.

top left: The designers gave the arms dealership simple, structured spaces with sealed cases of glass and gleaming matt steel, granite floors and a pared-down colour scheme of dark blues and greys; the whole is a deliberately impersonal environment.

above: Plan of sales area and showroom; the VIP room is on a floor below.

opposite: The sales and presentation area is dominated by a long, low counter in two-tone wood: the expense of the goods is emphasized by the rich materials used for the shop fittings.

Halfords Auto Depot

Swansea, Wales, UK, 1999
Interior Design: Ben Kelly Design

From punk designer to superstore outfitter – this is the somewhat unconventional career path followed by former art student Ben Kelly. In his mid-twenties he designed suitably yobbish shops and flats for Vivienne Westwood, Malcolm MacLaren and the Sex Pistols; after this he moved on to stylish night clubs and minimalist museum galleries; finally, in his fifties, he has found himself designing a new generation of mechanical superstores for the Halfords chain. Everything for the car, at a budget price and in large quantities, for ordinary consumers and motor enthusiasts – this was the marketing concept behind Auto Depot.

Outsider Kelly beat off competition from a number of established retail design companies with his effective mix of spare-part warehouse, glazed workshop and outsized, eye-catching typography. The radicalism of his design resides in an aesthetic approach which brilliantly organizes bare functionality into a total retail experience. 'Auto Depot was to employ a warehouse "no frills" feel in order to accommodate a very large range of products at lower prices. The design is functional and robust to complement the ethos of the project,' says Kelly.

Cost awareness is another striking feature of this design strategy. Plain glazed openings have been cut into the unornamented façade of the metal hangar, the endless rows of shelves assembled, with few modifications, from a widely available industrial shelving system. The choice of materials has been thoroughly pragmatic, too: zinc mesh, steel, wooden telegraph poles, factory flooring, and other very basic ingredients are put together to

above: The functional interior of the vast store resembles both a metal hangar and a no-nonsense warehouse, and is capable of housing a huge range of products at low cost to the consumer.

opposite: The Auto Depot combines spare-part warehouse and car workshop: the easily identified fitting bay, delineated by its corrugated steel cladding, is signposted by eye-catching, oversized typography.

create an authentically mechanical ambience for car fanatics. Such customers can watch through large windows while their treasured motor has its new exhaust fitted by specialists under the clinically bright lighting of the Fitting Bay or while their newly purchased tyres are put in place.

The first Auto Depots built to Kelly's blueprint were pilot projects in provincial locations. The second branch, which opened in Swansea in July 1999, covers 1,785 square metres – slightly more than the first one, based in Sheffield. It demonstrates even more clearly than its predecessor the seamless convergence of the architect's and the client's intentions. Halfords did well to opt for the no-nonsense approach of the one-time punk designer. This self-service paradise for car-lovers is totally down-to-earth, with no hint of artificial glamour – and so it is perfectly in tune with its customers, whose world begins and ends with their beloved vehicle.

top left: Exterior of the Auto Depot showing the main entrance and approach. Glazed areas, large graphic features, swathes of colour and cedar wood panelling animate the standard 'shed' façade.

above: The central corridor from the rear of the store shows Kelly's robust approach and use of materials: industrial shelving, telegraph pole supports and factory flooring, for example.

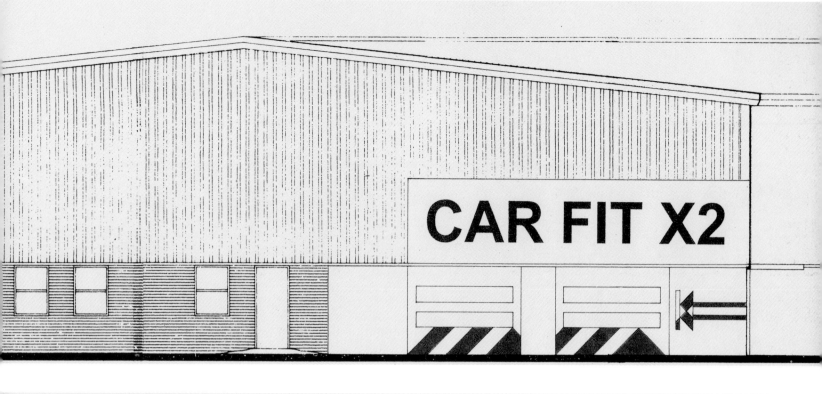

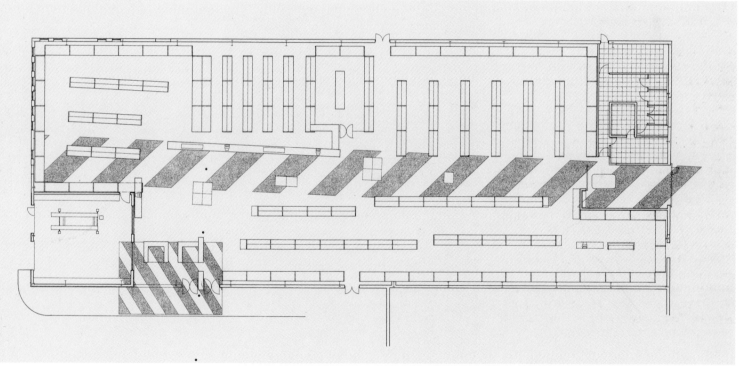

top: Elevation of the side of the building, again showing the use of oversized typography as a signpost.

above: Plan

Joseph Menswear

London, UK, 1997
Architecture / Interior Design:
David Chipperfield Architects

The name Joseph Ettedgui is closely associated with South Kensington's transformation into one of London's most fashionable shopping districts. In the early 1980s, his first fashion store provided the initial impetus for Terence Conran, Katharine Hamnett, Issey Miyake and other famous names to move into the neighbourhood. Soon there was not just one 'Joseph', but a number of them, all having one thing in common: a highly distinctive architectural style. The designers selected by entrepreneur Ettedgui for his stores were Norman Foster (pre-knighthood), Eva Jiricna and David Chipperfield. It was to the last of this trio that he entrusted his most recent project, which is also his first store devoted exclusively to men's fashions.

The 1960s building on Sloane Avenue had hitherto served the Joseph boss as a back office, housing his administrative departments on the second floor. Chipperfield took a radical approach to the job, tearing open the façade and completely emptying out the ground floor and the one above. The new glazed front of the store is two storeys high and the offices above this level are encased with a metal screen. The sales area is undivided, interrupted only by a regular grid pattern of concrete pillars and an elaborate double-helix spiral staircase connecting the two floors of the shop. All the necessary fixtures and fittings – changing

The splendid isolation of the minimalist store, perceived to appeal to sophisticated male consumers. A double-helix spiral staircase connects two floors of retail space.

rooms and clothes racks, for example – are made of wood, clearly standing out as additions against the light-coloured stone and the white of the pillars and ceilings.

The design celebrates the exclusive cult of minimalism: the obvious under-use of space and the small number of articles on display signal exclusivity, in a deliberate contrast to the fast-paced, over-the-top extravagance of the popular fashion chains. This austere style of presentation for upmarket stores is to some extent a phenomenon of the recent past, but given the store's target customer group this choice may well be the right one. Tasteful minimalism is the essence of sober masculinity. Men have always been more conservative as consumers, and so yesterday's fashions in women's retailing can still pass muster, even in more colourful times, for the male of the species.

above left: The opened-up glass and concrete façade of the store on Sloane Avenue – one of London's most exclusive shopping districts. The large entrance doors bear the company name with stylish understatement.

above: Sparse changing cubicles continue the minimalist theme of the boutique, but the use of wood creates a striking contrast to the predominant white of the ceilings and pillars.

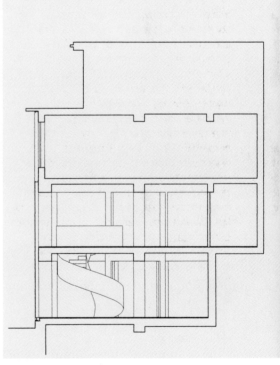

above: The upper floor,
with the curves of the
top of the staircase
contrasting with the
flat pillars and wide
panes of glass.

above: Section

More Moss

New York, New York, USA, 1999
Interior Design: Harry Allen & Associates

Murray Moss, one of the most endearing afficionados on the international design scene, expressed his passion for the finest things of contemporary life in the shopping space he created in New York in the mid-1990s, which he named, quite simply, after himself. But that was not enough: the 1999 offshoot, located in a neighbouring building, promises 'More Moss'.

This repository of everyday items is more than 600 square metres bigger than its predecessor and – most unusually for follow-ups – presents itself in far more uncompromising fashion, effectively in the style of a museum. The products are separated from their mundane functions and raised to the status of artefacts encased in glass display cases, some of which rotate. 'The systematic case systems and platforms allow for smaller or larger stories. The bays become the graphic division, much like pages in a magazine that organize the stories. Every product can be seen, desired, and ultimately purchased', explain the interior designers of Harry Allen & Associates, who also designed the first project in 1995. In front of the long wall show cases there are even the same metal rails that many museums use to keep visitors and exhibits at a safe distance from each other. Moss freely admits that he copied the diorama principle of the glass fronts set into the walls from natural history collections. He even takes the analogy so far as to include a few stuffed animals among the design objects. No-one before him has enacted the conceit of setting up commonplace objects as items for artistic contemplation in such brilliantly designed retail architecture.

On the other hand, aesthetic and even ideological blinkers are well in place here, shutting

above: Moss's original and idiosyncratic show cases are variations of those found in natural history museums – hence the stuffed animals – but the artefacts can, of course, be bought.

opposite: The museum motif of the show cases is further developed by the 'do not touch' rails. Harry Allen & Associates' scheme allowed the products to be organized in a systematic series of bays.

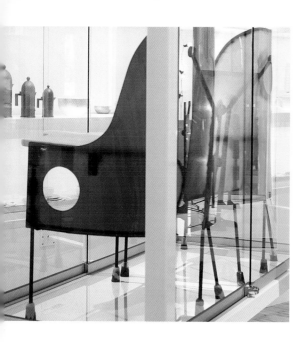

out the change in values which has taken hold of the design world during the transition to a new century. For neither exquisite designs nor higher meanings lie behind the democratization of everyday culture adopted as a strategy by such disparate characters as Philippe Starck and Jasper Morrison. Rather than mystifying the objects, they seek to do away with the idea of 'design' as a distancing attribute, creating a new and unproblematic user-object relationship. Intelligently designed products should be complete in themselves, they should be good value, and they should not have to display an awe-inspiring label marked 'design'. However, this presupposes a completely different concept of marketing from Moss's 'Do not touch – but do purchase' philosophy.

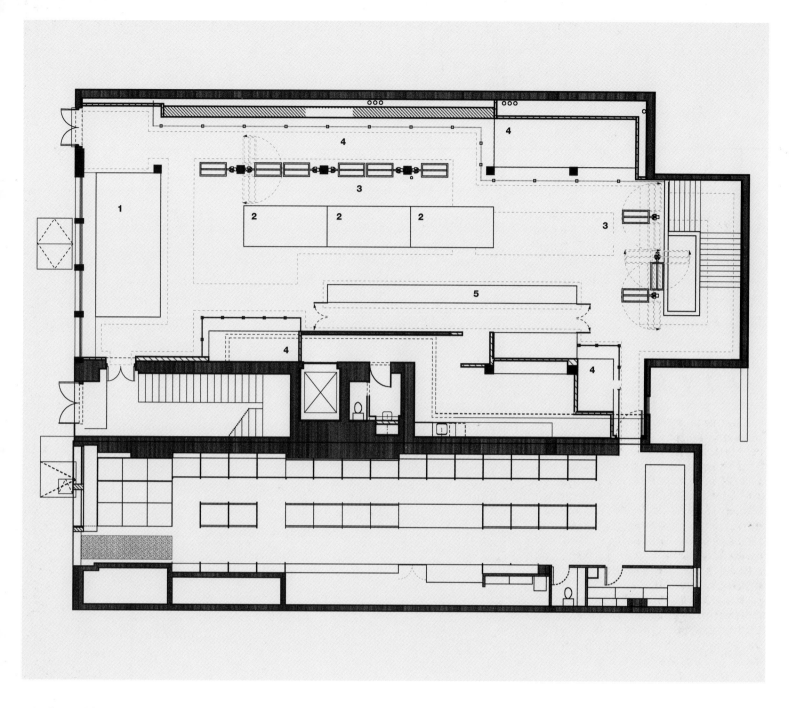

opposite, top left:
Chairs sit enshrined in
one of the numerous
glass cases.

opposite: By placing an
item such as this chair
designed by Jean
Nouvel on a platform,
it is positioned for
admiration rather than
trying out for size.

above: Plan
1 window display
  platform
2 platform
3 pivot cases
4 diorama
5 cash desk

Pronovias

Madrid, Spain, 1997
Interior Design: GCA Arquitectos

No chandeliers or stucco ceilings, no gold
borders, fancy mirrors or ornate furnishings. In
this bridal store everything is different: there is
not the slightest hint of ballroom kitsch or
romantic frippery anywhere. Probably no long-
established operator in this sector has broken
more radically with the industry's own stylistic
conventions than Madrid's high-profile bridal
company Pronovias. Behind the old shop
façade, decorated with wrought iron grilles,
visitors walk into a world of understated luxury:
a succession of rooms over two storeys in an
elegant and unfussy style that would grace the
showroom of a classic fashion brand is all the
more astonishing in a setting designed for
lavish festive finery.

   GCA Arquitectos from Barcelona was
commissioned with this conversion project.
The ground floor – 30 metres deep – presented a rather awkward situation in design terms:
to overcome this the designers divided up the
space by varying the floor level. From the
street, three steps lead up to the glazed
entrance; four more steps at the end of the
reception area lead to a central platform, which
has a spacious, light stairway leading to the
upper storey and which also gives access to
the sales rooms at the rear of the ground floor.
In all, the store has 600 square metres of
useable floor space, two thirds of which is located in the upper storey. 'The most important

**An old building was
given an interesting spatial
redesign by varying the
floor level: steps lead up to
the ground floor from the
entrance and up again to
the central platform with
its glazed stairway.**

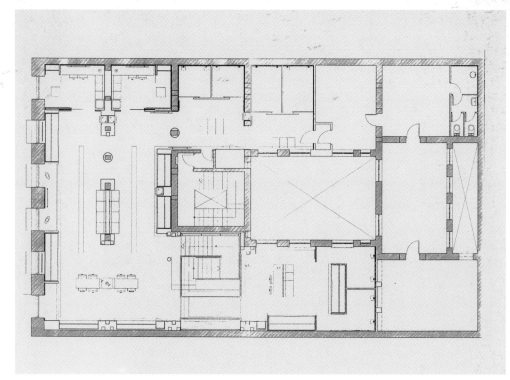

objective of the project was to create a neutral and homogeneous setting, focused on the presentation and requirements of the products – with the goal of making the bride the sole protagonist': this is how the designers describe their strategy, and they made good use of the freedom given to them in every respect, creating a concept that is consistent and persuasive right down to the very last detail.

Inside, groups of black-and-white photographs are the only visible reference to the nature of the business; the gowns themselves remain hidden behind sliding partitions or shrouded in protective bags. Spacious changing facilities provide ample room for trying on the costly garments; outside, escorts can prepare to deliver their verdict from luxurious padded seating. Any additional discussions and decision-making processes are conducted at well-proportioned conference tables made of light-coloured wood. Here there is absolutely nothing to get in the way of what is rarely a simple purchasing decision. Whether she is bride, bridesmaid or belle of the ball – the customer will feel in good hands in this ambience of resolute profession-alism, for she alone is the focus of attention, able to take time and good advice to choose the garments which will make her a sensation on the day.

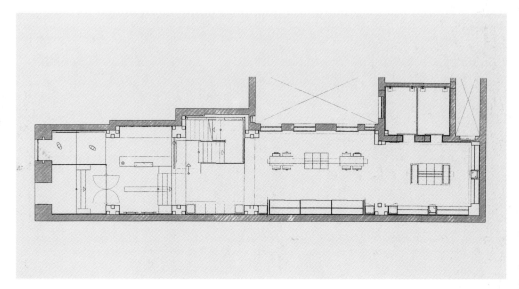

top left: The neutral colour scheme is enhanced by light-coloured furniture and diffused lighting – all conducive to providing a calm atmosphere. Wedding gowns are hidden behind protective partitions.

top: Plan of the large first floor

above: Plan of the ground floor

opposite: Spacious and luxurious padded seating arrangements enable the customer (and entourage) to choose gowns at her leisure.

opposite and above: Pale wood tables and leather-and-steel chairs provide business-like settings for client-staff discussions. Occasional bridal photographs are the only real hints of the nature of the business; the store's clean lines and ambient atmosphere are the antithesis of matrimonial fussiness.

Sirius Smart Sounds

Maastricht, The Netherlands, 1997
Interior Design: Maurice Mentjens

It is not just that many of those substances which are so assiduously pursued by the authorities elsewhere are legally permitted in The Netherlands – in other ways, too, this small and liberal country has a uniquely open-minded outlook, receptive to new trends and fashions. Since the boom in club culture, with its techno, house and jungle music, the haze-filled coffee shops and musty hippy stores have become seriously un-cool for young consumers. The alternative was not long in coming: since 1995, the Sirius Smart Shops have established a chain of branches across three Dutch cities.

As their name suggests, these stores offer smart products – from energy drinks and body-building foods through to stimulants, of the natural and not-so-natural varieties, and pounding music: in short, everything to make style-conscious hearts beat faster, and in some cases more healthily. This is not the place for anyone who thinks that Fast Forward, Eclipse, Kryptonite, Explore, HomE, G-Spot, Remedy, Vinyl and Drum'n Bass sound like a range of household cleaning products. Not only the merchandise but even the design of the Smart Shops is modelled on 'the most important elements of house culture: music, dance, ecstasy, smart drugs, technology, virtuality,

With its block-like counter-and-playdeck structures, this 'techno temple' is designed to vibrate with bass rhythms. Behind the counter is a grid of connectors displaying new releases; the dark back room is called the 'catacomb'.

spirituality'. For interior designer and store fitter Maurice Mentjens, who has created all the Sirius stores to date, these are not just words, but a design credo he has demonstrated in a new and unique way with each successive project.

His first creation was an alchemist's laboratory, the second he dubbed a 'smart chapel', then came a holographic cabinet of wall hangings – and the fourth, Sirius Smart Sounds, is a 'techno temple' vibrating to the pounding rhythms of the bass sound. The floor is peppered with loudspeakers emitting rumbling archaic rhythms; according to Mentjens, 'it is a metaphor for the heartbeat of the earth'. Or for an earthquake, perhaps? Certainly this is how it looks: the fittings consist of block-like shapes, set at odd angles, all made of aluminium. Changing light effects produce iridescent colours on the shimmering metal surfaces of the walls and ceilings.

The shop consists of two rooms, measuring 70 square metres in all; the rear one, the gloomier of the two, is called the 'catacomb'. Although the budgets have risen from one store to the next – making Smart Sounds was the most expensive Sirius store thus far – the project was hardly an excessive one in financial terms. The interior decor of this techno-temple cost all of EUR 52,000.

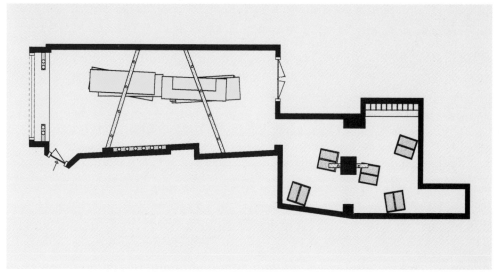

above: Plan of the two rooms

above and opposite,
top: The shimmering
surfaces serve as
perfect screens for the
varying colours of the
changing lights.

Waterstone's

Piccadilly, London, UK, 1999
Interior Design: BDG McColl
Layout: Waterstone's
Architecture: John Strong & Partners

The point-of-no-return has a date and a name. Since newcomer Jeff Bezos in Seattle started up his amazon.com website, initially the subject of some ridicule, nothing has been quite the same in the traditional book retailing world. Just as female warriors of Homerian sagas created havoc among the macho world of heroes, so this agile new combatant has thrown the book business into confusion.

The mechanisms of the mail order business were nothing new, but the fact that ordering at the click of a mouse generated a completely unexpected dynamic and turned the entire industry upside down in America and Europe, is one of the true wonders of the digital age. Just when booksellers had become more or less accustomed to the parallel universe of electronic media and incorporated these in their product range, they now had to face up to a fleet-footed cyberspace competitor in the global marketplace. This could easily mean the end for many small bookshops; as for the major players, they are resorting to a single strategic weapon: size. More surface area, books and service is their recipe for success. The aim is for readers to immerse themselves in a total retail experience where browsing, rummaging and relaxing combine to create a single inspiring event which beats surfing at home.

This concept has been taken furthest by British book retailing chain Waterstone's.

The ground floor of the shop retains some of the modernist feel of the previous Daks Simpsons store, but, overwhelmingly, presents a contemporary treasure trove library of books.

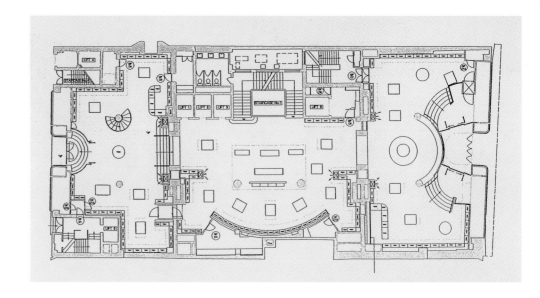

Following a few notable new projects outside London, the company opened Europe's biggest ever book bazaar there in 1999. The location is top-drawer: Waterstone's moved into the former premises of clothing department store Simpsons, which had been based on Piccadilly since 1930. Over eight storeys with a total sales area of 6,130 square metres, the store houses 265,000 books, a gift shop, an art gallery, a 175-seat auditorium, internet terminals, and four restaurants and bars.

BDG McColl, in collaboration with Waterstone's, designed this mega-store. On the Piccadilly site, the existing layout of the building provided an opportunity to follow the traditional department-store principle of allocating particular product categories to different floors, applying this to the various categories of the book market. Each storey opens up a different literary world – from non-fiction to fiction and poetry, the arts, and specialist literature. Distinctive features of the former fashion department store, such as the marble staircase and the walls of glass blocks were retained, otherwise the interior designers focused on producing a modern, minimalist interpretation of an old paradigm – the library as a treasure trove of knowledge and pleasure. Any impression of aggressive marketing is avoided, in favour of foregrounding the encounter with books, the allure of reading. There are leather armchairs everywhere, inviting visitors to linger. The message of the project as a whole is unmistakable and entirely in tune with Waterstone's objectives: 'amplifying its existing strengths, such as high levels of service and an obvious passion for books' (BDG McColl).

top: Plan of the ground floor – the layout for the ground floor was conceived by the Waterstone's in-house design team.

above: The children's section on the second floor benefits from a brightly decorated play/learn interactive area with seating pods and a juice bar close at hand.

**Designers' sketch of
the colourful lounge
area with its writing
surfaces and comfort-
able seating, situated
on the third floor.**

SIXTH FLOOR
WHAT'S ON?
THE EVENT FLOOR

FIFTH FLOOR
PHOTOGRAPHY, DESIGN,
ARCHITECTURE AND
ALL THE ARTS

FOURTH FLOOR
LOOKING FOR KNOWLEDGE?
ACADEMIC &
PROFESSIONAL

THIRD FLOOR
COOKING, GARDENING,
SELF HELP, SPORTS AND MORE
LIFESTYLE & LEISURE

SECOND FLOOR
ALL ABOUT
CHILDREN & LEARNING

FIRST FLOOR
PURE FICTION
THE FACT IS WE HAVE MORE THAN
ANY OTHER BOOKSHOP

HERE AND NOW
BESTSELLERS, NEW
REVIEWED, PEOPLE
& TRAVEL

LOWER GROUND FLOOR
ANYTHING ELSE YOU NEED?
NEWS & MAGAZINES, GIFTS
& CUSTOMER SERVICES

FIFTH FLOOR
GREAT VIEWS, GREAT
DRINKS. RELAX WITH A
BOOK ON THE SIDE
LOUNGE-BAR

FOURTH FLOOR
BROWSE AROUND THE
WORLD ON THE
INTERNET STATION

SECOND FLOOR
COOL & FUN – WHAT
BETTER WAY TO DO
YOURSELF SOME GOOD
JUICE BAR

LOWER GROUND FLOOR
BREAKFAST, LUNCH
AND DINNER, YOU CAN
EAT YOUR WAY THROUGH
THE DAY IN THE
RESTAURANT
OR CAFE

BOOKS, FOOD & DRINK
FOR EVERY TASTE

opposite: Bold primary colour schemes and strong shapes for store furniture create a memorable impact and cohesive design schema. An abundance of soft leather sofas invite the customer to take his or her time when choosing a book.

above: Strong, colourful signage on the ground floor helps orientate customers and presents the wide array of choice available – both literary and edible – without overwhelming them.

Zero Lustrum Pukeberg

Stockholm, Sweden, 1999
Interior Design: Rupert Gardner Design

Three established Swedish brands selling glass accessories, lighting and furnishings joined forces to create a sales and display outlet in Stockholm's city centre. The companies commissioned local architects Rupert Gardner Design, with the brief that they should organize the different product areas effectively, as well as creating the requisite internal flexibility to make this synthesis of retail business, gallery and showroom into an effective attraction for a wide variety of consumers. Rupert Gardner said: 'The goal was to make the three companies really visible, to make the companies more available to the public. Our concept was to draw people inside by creating a progression, from the "soft" home-interior pieces up front to the "industrial" bookshelves at the back.'

The 820 square metres of useable floor-space extends backwards from the entrance on the street to a depth of 60 metres. Two completely contrasting types of wall design ensure that the route consumers follow to reach the distant areas is constantly interesting. On the left-hand side, strikingly illuminated glass products are set in front of a wall made of Nordic pine with a horizontal relief pattern; on the opposite side is a long, back-lit wall of light with metal boards which changes colour every fifteen minutes. The designers have placed a small, circular office area where the space widens out; behind this, an L-shaped annexe linked to the main building houses the gallery, with temporary displays, and the furniture and lighting departments.

A high degree of flexibility is an inherent feature of this design. Sliding walls and mobile glass partitions allow for the space to be arranged in many different ways. A video

above: Effectively lit glassware is displayed on shelves incorporated into the horizontal pattern of the Nordic pine wall.

opposite: The shop – a showcase for three companies – extends back 60 metres from the entrance; the route towards the rear is kept lively with a variety of coloured lighting and interesting structural shapes.

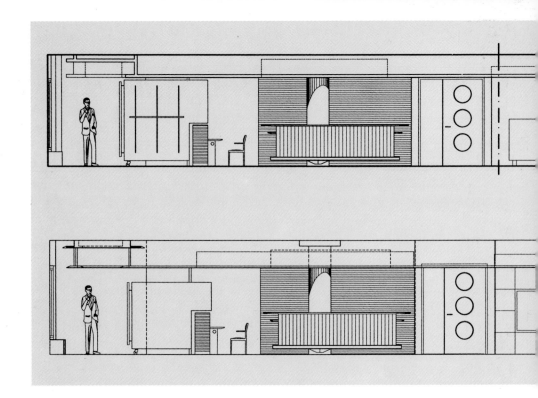

projection screen is concealed behind the bright red back wall which ends the narrow front sales area. The vast diversity of lighting solutions and the range of contrasting materials used are central to the overall impression and the effective way visitors are led through the building. Sandstone, mosaics, bare concrete and untreated wood, together with the sculpted ceiling with its multitude of different light sources, create a perfect setting for the panorama of beautiful objects which are on display.

above: The varied colour scheme throughout the store is apparent not only in the floor and wall surfaces but also in the typography on the glass partitions.

top and above:
Sections showing the
division of spaces and
partitions, and the
circulation area.

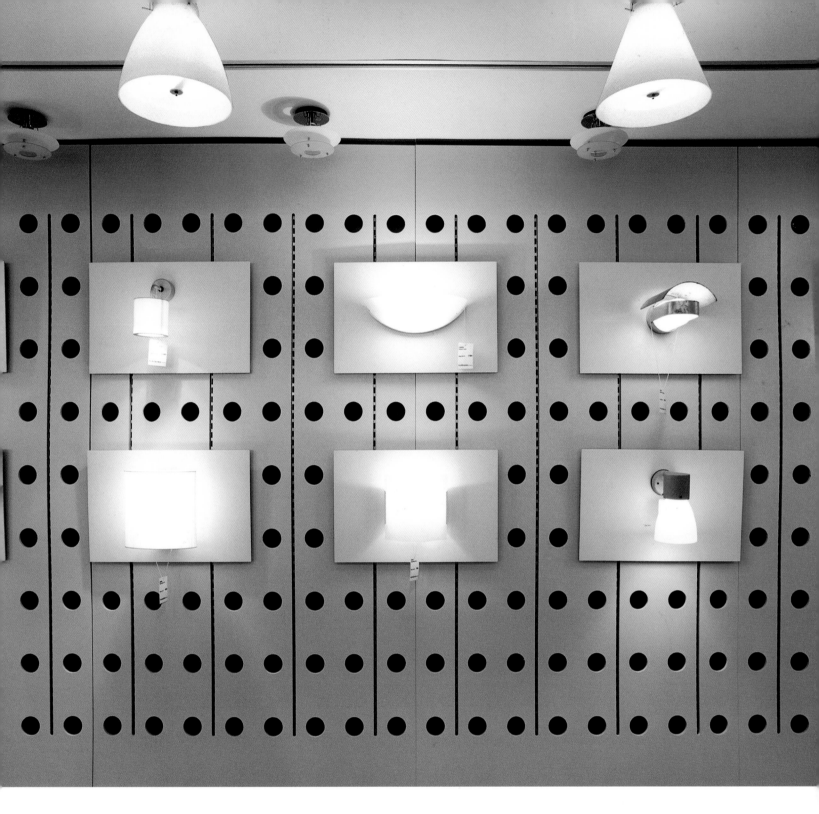

opposite: The diversity of materials, lighting sources and choice of colours is apparent in the lively ceiling design and supporting pillars: cobalt-blue mosaics provide a rich contrast to untreated wood, for example.

above: Flexibility is one of the key elements in the design of the store: displays of lighting such as this can be moved into any desired formation, and the backdrop is markedly different to the pine wall and shelves elsewhere.

Alan Journo

Milan, Italy, 1999
Interior Design: Ron Arad Associates

Ron Arad's name is emblematic of the exciting years when defamiliarized everyday objects were accorded the status of objets d'art, when design became a cult word and the latest creations found their way straight into collections and auction houses. The gifted London steelsmith and metal worker named his first workshop retail business One Off – and the creations he rivetted and welded together were indeed one-offs, a world away from industrial mass-production. Today the man who was once a hot tip on the fringe of the art world has become established as one of the uncontested greats of contemporary design. Arad made the transition from experimental to establishment with admirable integrity: driven by an irresistible, manic-organic compulsion to de-form his materials he did not let himself become distracted from his own artistic purposes in his collaborations with 'Zeitgeist' companies such as Kartell, Moroso or Vitra.

His design strategy was the same when it came to architecture. His own studio in Camden Town, London, was his apprenticeship piece; his design for the foyer of the new opera house in Tel Aviv took things a stage further; other projects, such as the studio building for a German publisher, were not carried out. And then there was the tiny fashion boutique in Milan's glamorous Via della Spiga.

Michelle ma Belle – named after the Beatles hit – was the title of this one-off walk-in sculpture created on an area of 6.6 metres by 5.3 metres in 1993. 'The Opera building had already been designed, the shop tried some of the same forms, but we had never seen the white curved walls with holes, and saw how it looked in an "arte povera" version. In

above: Ron Arad used all the conceivable space available when refurbishing the basement of the small, exclusive boutique: the walls of the staircase itself are utilized as display areas.

opposite: The exquisite stairway is a sculptural wrought steel garland descending from a double-pear-shaped opening above.

the Opera there was a process of obsessive drawing that left nothing for interpretation. Michelle ma Belle was looser,' Arad said.

Six years later, when the opportunity came up to add the basement as a further sales area, Arad set to work again. The result was no straightforward extension: the boutique – now trading under the name Alan Journo – was comprehensively redesigned. Its central feature is the staircase leading from the ground floor to the basement. An ordinary flight of stairs would have taken up far too much of the small space available, so Arad used the entire layout of the shop to provide the necessary access. The expensive garb is presented on four platforms along the stairway, which winds around a central opening in a double pear shape. In his Neal Street, London, shop design of 1984 Arad had already demonstrated how effective a sculpturally-designed stairway could be as an architectural focal point. The unending garland of the banister of wrought steel in Alan Journo also offers a variation on a theme of one of Arad's most famous designs, the Well Tempered Chair of 1986. Part of the genius of Ron Arad is his ability to paraphrase his own designs effectively, here in a majestic and distinctive solution to a tricky spatial situation.

The walls are fitted with recesses on a diagonal grid pattern which allow the hanging rails to be easily reorganized.

The rhythm of the grand staircase's undulating loops is echoed in the repetition of the curves of the floors.

Virmani Fashion Shop

Munich, Germany, 1998
Interior Design: Design Associates

Munich-based designers Stephen Lang and Uwe Binnberg of Design Associates were commissioned to devise a scheme for this high-class clothing retailer in their home town. With the brief to showcase a fashion range that spoke instantly of its exclusivity, within a relatively small space, many would have opted for a purely minimalist aesthetic. However, the designers sought to combine a modern, clean interior with lively and unusual details, reflecting something of the Indian ethnicity of the client and a real feeling for different materials; Lang and Binnberg's philosophy is that 'fashion sells by emotion', so they sought to produce a cool space with a sensual side, which reflected the garments on display.

The volume of the 120-square-metre shop floor is divided up to accommodate the main boutique, along with changing rooms, storage space and an office; the floor level is raised at the rear to add further variation to the space. The left hand wall, which runs almost the entire length of the shop, is successfully used as a display area with elegant S-shaped steel and brass hanging rails protruding at intervals from rows of brass wall studs which also allow for light teak shelves to be positioned at different levels as needed. Both straight and undulating lines of pebble-mosaics set into the concrete slab floor echo the form and rhythm of the rails and rail-ends and draw the eye eventually to an antique Indian wooden door at the rear of the boutique. Elsewhere, a rich combination of materials is also deployed: four limestone steps on the right hand side of the shop, stripped antique-wood columns and two elegant double-disc pendant lights designed by Catallani and Smith.

above: Four antique limestone steps lead from the front of the shop to the raised rear section and provide contrast to the other plain surfaces.

opposite: S-shaped brass-tipped steel rods create unusual – and artistic – features of the humble shop clothes rail; the eye is led to another rich feature: the old stripped door at the back of the store.

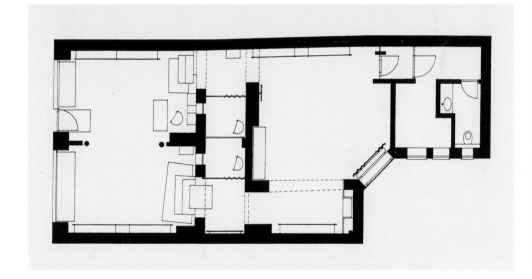

White plaster walls, carefully positioned spotlights and two large plate glass street-front windows decorated only by the Virmani name and offset with a few modest mannequins, do – for all the fine detailing – of course still convey a minimalist message. But the achievement of the design is that combination of forces which give it real individuality in a cool setting; as a result, the clothes can speak for themselves without the intrusion of extraneous clutter, and also convey their own particular identity. In turn, the customer benefits from a feeling of brand identification and loyalty and a sense of shopping exclusivity – a heady combination.

top: The two large windows of the shop façade allow clear views beyond the mannequins into the elegant interior.

above: Floor plan

The concrete floor is decorated with straight and swirling lines of pebble mosaic which echo the rhythm of the garment rails along the wall.

Hushush

Tokyo, Japan, 2000
Interior Design: Harry Allen & Associates

A handful of Japanese and international design companies were invited to enter the competition to develop a suitable retail setting for a new brand collection. Hushush, a range of 'basic' fashions, wanted to create a distinctive impact from the outset through its architectural presentation. The test site was a retail outlet of just under 500 square metres in the Kouhoku New Town district of Tokyo and the proposal by winning company Harry Allen & Associates, was anything but pretentious: 'The challenge to provide a backdrop for a brand of basic clothing has never been met with a successful solution. No matter how hard designers have tried to be "basic", they cannot help styling the concept. But "basic" is not a style, it is a reality. And consumers are ready to accept reality. Forget ergonomics and tasteful styling. Like a minimalist sculpture, the concept will focus on materials and geometry,' Allen said.

These interior designers had achieved recognition in New York primarily for their austere manifesto designs for Murray Moss, and in Japan they were no less rigorous in their approach. The Hushush store layout is designed on a basic model of large-scale wall sections forming a diagonal grid pattern on the floor. These wall sections fulfil all the necessary functions: they are used as storage,

The cosmetics area is defined by bold use of reflective stainless steel; the oversized blood-red letters of the store name add decorative effect to cabinets and walls.

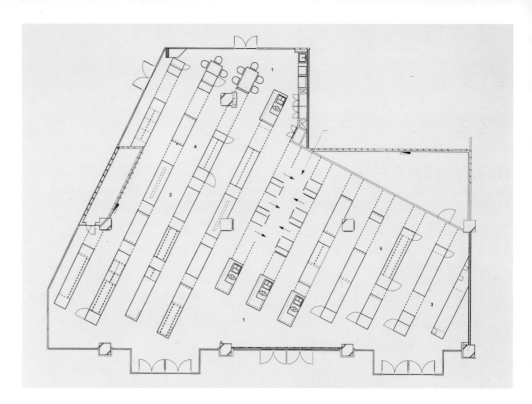

merchandise display areas, cash desk, changing room and signposting system in one. Different surface materials are allocated to different product groups to guide customers through the modules – of which there are eleven in all, each around one metre deep and up to eighteen metres long. Cement stands for Basic, mirrors for Trendy, black panelling for children's fashions, stainless steel for cosmetics, acrylic for accessories, plywood for the cash desk and the café. Varying heights, gaps and open shelf or hanging systems allow customers to see through from one area into another.

The designers do not deny that the idea of the rigid lengthways division is borrowed from the standard supermarket design repertoire. In their eyes this underpins what they proclaim as their new honesty in presenting basic branded fashions. The trick here is that something ordinary is transformed into something out of the ordinary, that a familiar scenario unfolds surprising spatial qualities – while at the same time remaining what retail design must primarily be: a vehicle for displaying merchandise and not self-regarding, an end in itself.

top: Floor plan.
1 **Cash/wrap (plywood)**
2 **Accessories (acrylic)**
3 **Cosmetics (stainless steel)**
4 **Trendy (mirrors)**
5 **Basics (concrete)**

above: The changing cubicles are are kept simple using a combination of minimalist concrete and mirrors – padded cushions allow a little bit of comfort.

Concrete is used as the
main material in the
Basic clothing area; the
designers' focus on
honest geometry, as
well as materials, is
enhanced by repetition
of form.

opposite: Looking from
the children's depart-
ment towards the cash
and wrap area shows
the use of plywood as a
defining material.

above: The large plate
glass windows of the
store front allow views
into the brightly lit
interior from the mall
walkway at night.

chapter three shopping as leisure

Markets, shopping centres and mega-malls
When Karl Marx prophesied that one day, after the age of necessity, the kingdom of freedom would dawn in the highly developed capitalist nations, he could not have suspected how radically his prediction would be fulfilled in the outgoing twentieth century. Wage slavery, and the dominance of the majority by a wealthy minority, were not yet things of the past, but the old-style industrial society had certainly had its day. Abandoned factory sites reflect the decline of entire industries. Labouring jobs are becoming scarce while the services industry booms. Where these derelict industrial properties have not been razed to the ground they are steadily being taken over by new occupants. The huge walls and spaces provide a suitably dramatic backdrop for new retail facilities and a great deal else besides. Even grandiose railway buildings are being transformed into shopping centres: where once only passengers jostled towards the trains there are now hordes of strolling shoppers. Mixed uses are becoming the order of the day, yielding apparently unlimited permutations of retail, entertainment and service products. The post-modern precept of 'learning from Las Vegas' has been thoroughly absorbed by developers and designers, who are showing in ever more hybrid mega projects how effectively they have learned their lesson when it comes to entertainment architecture. But it is inherent to the dialectic of fun architecture that architecture itself makes a comeback just when you least expect it – when supermarkets and shopping centres in such diverse locations as Miami Beach and Salzburg become genuine architectural attractions.

opposite: The bold, swirling roof structure of Eric Kuhne's Bluewater shopping centre in Kent, UK, indicates the confidence and aspirations behind the building of the mega-malls.

Bluewater

Dartford, UK, 1999
Architecture: Eric Kuhne & Associates

American architect Eric Kuhne worked with Michael Graves, the high priest of postmodern architecture, for long enough to be able to make even a secular commission for a huge shopping mall into something special, true to the spirit of Graves's own eclectic catechism with a suitable profusion of historical quotations and references. This architectural excess fitted perfectly with the client's own aspirations.

Australian property company Land Lease, which operates shopping complexes worldwide, wanted its first European project to set new standards for the genre: the largest ever shopping centre in the old world, representing an investment of EUR 1.8 billion, with 140,000 square metres of usable floor space, was also to set a new benchmark in terms of architectural quality. And the project does indeed present successful, imaginative solutions based on tried and tested formulae. The two-storey shopping arcades (total length: more than 500 metres) are arranged in a triangle around the parking decks. The three prime corner sites are occupied by branches of major department stores, and in total Bluewater accommodates 320 individual shops and restaurants. Each of the three pedestrianized areas is designed as a 'village' with a particular theme: the eastern one is popular and family-centred, the southern one focuses on the younger generation with entertainment products and media stores and

Kuhne's postmodern glass and steel forms are playfully illuminated at night; the glazed construction is the biggest in Britain since the great Victorian palm houses of Kew Gardens.

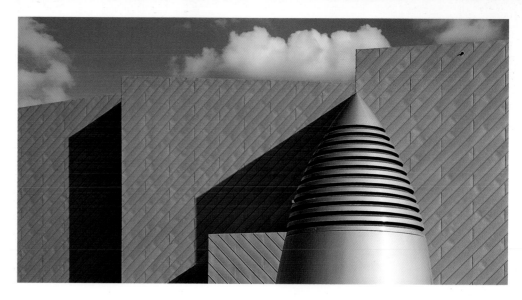

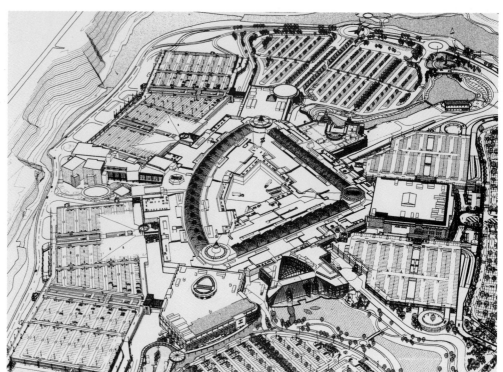

the western one brings together designer brands and gourmet eateries.

'We've really designed a city rather than a retail destination', emphasizes Kuhne, and because 'modernism eradicated the identity of civilizations and robbed architecture of its story-telling quality', he compensates for this loss with a multitude of motifs and reminiscences from architectural history and beyond. The Winter Garden in the western food court – claiming to be the largest constructed in England in the twentieth century – is reminis-cent of Decimus Burton's Palm House in Kew Gardens. Ornamental domed atria elsewhere in the huge complex pay homage to Sir John Soanes and Karl Friedrich Schinkel. Literary quotations from authors including Charles Dickens, Rudyard Kipling and Vita Sackville-West are emblazoned on friezes – the only common factor apparently being that these authors all resided in the area around the present-day Bluewater site: in the middle of an abandoned limestone quarry in Kent, close to the M2 motorway.

This rough scar in the gentle hills of Kent forms a dramatic backdrop for the mega-mall – and the project's real architectural achievement is arguably the way it skilfully turns this location to its advantage. The rockfaces which surround the buildings effectively counteract the huge masses of the complex itself, and the lavish landscaping – with numerous water features (including a 2.3 hectare lake) and tree-lined approach avenues – interweaves the new design with its existing environment.

top: A conical turret is imaginatively set against the backdrop of strong rectangular forms – the centre sets a new benchmark for shopping malls in terms of architectural quality as much as size.

above The vast complex is situated in an abandoned quarry carved out of the gentle Kent hills; skill-ful landscaping has harmoniously linked the centre to its natural environment.

The interior is a 'city' of themed shopping, with major department stores forming the anchors at three prime corner sites reached by two-storey, balconied arcades; architectural features such as large, airy domes provide architectural nuance.

Friedrichstadt Passagen

Berlin, Germany, 1997
Architecture: Oswalt Mathias Ungers /
Pei, Cobb, Freed & Partners
Interior Design: Calvin Tsao

The decision to fill three entire blocks with major new constructions on the most prominent section of the Friedrichsstrasse, once a famous shopping street, dates from the last days of socialist town planning, when the authorities wanted to do everything possible to elevate the eastern half of Berlin to the status of a global metropolis. After the end of the GDR, this mega-project fell into the lap of investor groups who were keen to retain its ambitious scale, but decided to engage top international names for the architecture. The group of architectural creations which resulted is extremely diverse: all they have in common is the height of their eaves and their mix of uses – retail and catering spaces, up to seven storeys of offices and a top storey with penthouse apartments.

The familiar rigid grid patterning of Oswalt Mathias Ungers dominates Quartier 205; New York architects Pei, Cobb, Freed & Partners dressed their Quartier 206 with a jagged, back-lit Art Deco façade; and Jean Nouvel concealed Quartier 207 behind an opaque glass skin that curves upwards and away at the top. The Berlin branch of Parisian department store Galeries Lafayette opened in Nouvel's Quartier in early 1996. In the other blocks, trading under the single brand name Friedrichstadt Passagen, suitable tenants were a long time coming. Finally, the wife of one of the investors bravely made a virtue of necessity and founded her own designer department store in Quartier 206, where the entire 7,200 square metres of retail floorspace stood empty. The store interior was designed by old hand Calvin Tsao, whose earlier high-profile projects included the World of Joyce department store in Bangkok.

above: The Friedrichstrasse was once a famous shopping street in pre-war Berlin; after the fall of the wall, three international architects designed the (from foreground to background) Quartiers 205, 206 and 207 blocks in highly diverse styles.

opposite: A powerful sculpture made from compressed car metal by the artist John Chamberlain dominates the central atrium of Quartier 205.

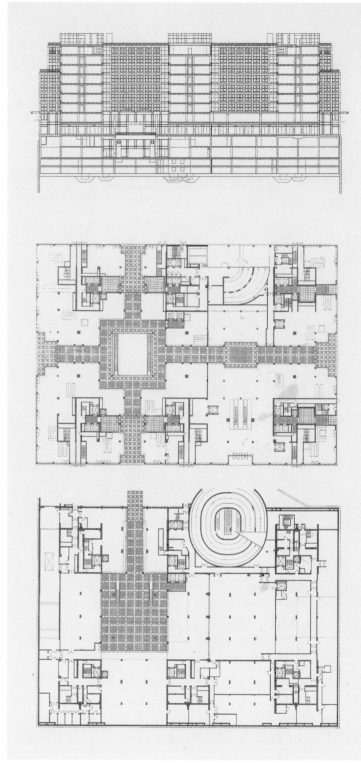

top and above: The
rigid grid architecture
of Oswalt Mathias
Ungers' Quartier 205
creates a powerful
presence on the street
corner, and the
entrance is clearly
indicated by a protrud-
ing canopy which
continues the pattern.

above: Quartier 205
section (top), plan of
first floor (centre) and
plan of basement
(bottom).

The central atrium of
Quartier 205 with its
escalator diagonals,
plain white walls and
minimalist furnishings
is made less austere by
the brilliant artworks.

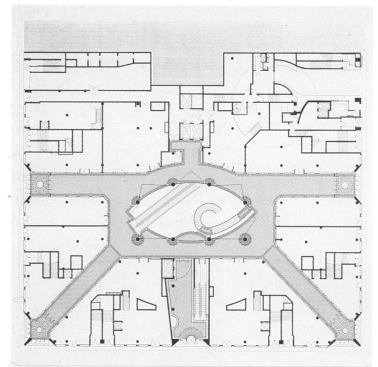

Since autumn 1997 there has been finally been life in the atrium, with its splendid Venetian mosaics and post-modern ornamentation. Quartier 205, where a monumental sculpture made of compressed car metal by John Chamberlains, standing in the austere square of the air well, provides a perhaps unintentional reminder of the transience of fashions and consumer goods, celebrated its opening at the same time, even though not all the sixty stores and units (covering 17,000 square metres in all) had been leased.

Both Ungers and his New York colleagues at Pei, Cobb, Freed & Partners attempted, in their individual vocabularies, to redefine the conventional urban block structure using the contradictory formula of maximum usage of space, profitable mix of tenants and expansion of the urban space. They were seeking to create 'a complementary space, a song, an event, a performance' (Pei, Cobb, Freed & Partners), to 'transform a traditional theme' (Ungers).

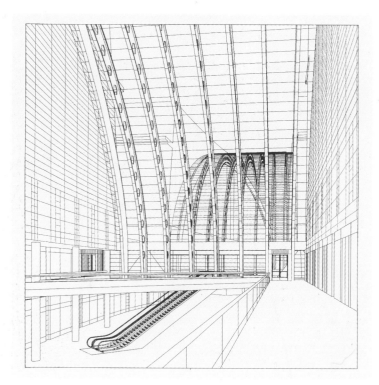

top left: Pei Cobb Freed & Partners created a jagged Art Deco façade for Quartier 206.

top: Plan of Quartier 206.

above: Section of Quartier 206 from the first floor, showing the arc of the atrium and descending escalators.

The highly decorative
interior of Quartier 206
is alive with postmodern
ornamentation, and the
swirling staircase is
artfully juxtaposed
against the escalators.

Vasco da Gama

Lisbon, Portugal, 1999
Architecture: Building Design
Partnership

The Portuguese capital used the international exposition EXPO 1998 as an opportunity to undertake a general architectural renewal of its urban infrastructure. One of the most prestigious projects was the development of the area lying between the EXPO railway station (Oriente), a spectacular design by Spanish architect Santiago Calatrava, and the actual exhibition site. In keeping with the oceanic theme of the event the gigantic shopping complex was named after the great explorer Vasco da Gama.

Unfortunately, delays resulted in the regrettable circumstance that crowds of EXPO visitors had to walk through an impressive but empty shell. The shopping centre, which cost EUR 92 million, did not officially open until 1999, a year later than scheduled. The competition for this prominent location, held in the run-up to the exposition, had been won by the major Iberian investment company Sonae Imobillária with a design by British architects Building Design Partnership. The client's goals were clear: 'To achieve the maximum retail, leisure, residential and parking possible within the EXPO 98 Competition Brief' (Building Design Partnership).

It speaks volumes for the creativity and professionalism of the architects, who had

The shopping centre, lying between Oriente railway station and the Lisbon EXPO centre, was treated as a three-storey walkway with interconnecting passageways and a filigree glass roof by British architects BDP.

previously completed a series of successful mall projects in the UK and elsewhere, that they were able to devise a unique solution of outstanding quality for this maritime setting. The almost square-shaped plot is cut through the middle by a wide, three-storey walkway, spanned by the filigree structures of the glass roof, which is 150 metres long and 30 metres wide. The rows of shops on the two upper storeys are connected by footbridges paved with glass slabs. The centre has a total retail area of 47,500 square metres, along with a multiplex cinema, a variety of catering establishments, and a suitably nautical sundeck. And there is an even better view for the tenants of the two stylish, 24-storey residential towers flanking the Vasco da Gama Centre, which will finally be ready for occupation in 2002.

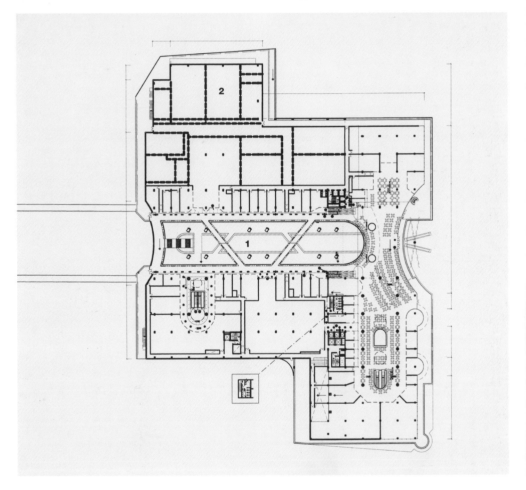

top left: The entrance to the centre fronts onto its maritime setting engagingly, with its billowing-sail-like overhanging roof and nautical-looking sun-deck cafe.

top right: The model shows the length of the 150 metres-long and 30 metres-wide mall and one of the two neighbouring residential towers, due for occupation in 2002.

**above: Plan of the ground floor
1 main mall
2 multiplex cinema**

The rows of shops on the upper levels are dramatically connected by walkways – echoing ship gangways – made of glass slabs and curvaceous railings.

Publix on the Bay

Miami Beach, Florida, USA, 1998
Architecture: Wood and Zapata

Publix, founded in 1930, is one of the top ten supermarket companies in the USA, with annual sales in excess of US$ 13 billion. The company's founder George W. Jenkins took the name from a chain of cinemas which has long since fallen into oblivion, and today the retail giant, which is majority-owned by its own employees, is a leading force in the south-eastern states and especially in Florida. Publix has achieved commercial success and a strong reputation for its value-for-money strategy and the high quality of its products and services – but scarcely for its architecture, which is thoroughly conventional: business is conducted in the usual box-type construction draped with a decorative façade to match the particular retail park in which it is set.

This, at least, is how it used to be, and whether the spectacular exception in Miami Beach becomes the norm still remains to be seen. Perhaps it was something in the air of the place – where candy-coloured art deco splendour and stylish contemporary design provide a popular setting for a booming fashion and entertainment scene – which prompted Publix to go for the grand architectural gesture. Although, in fact, the company was compelled to deviate from its habitual concept by the relatively small size of the commercial plot

The dramatically sweeping curves of the supermarket façade are designed to make a statement and also facilitate the creation of ramps to take shoppers with trolleys to car parking on the roof level.

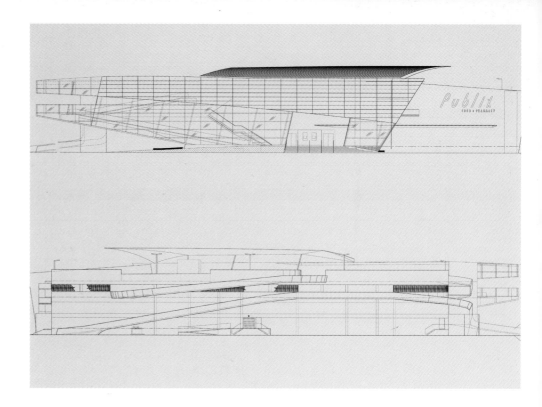

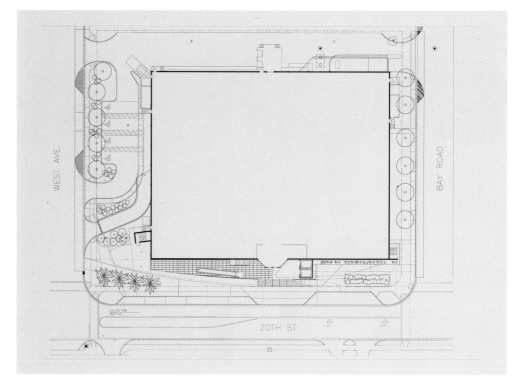

(previously occupied by the local electricity company) which did not leave enough space for parking around the supermarket itself (covering nearly 4,500 square metres). This practical constraint was the starting point from which Boston-based architects Wood and Zapata conjured up their spectacular creation, setting the parking decks on top of the box and adding boldly-curved ramps to connect the parking facilities with the store itself. Dramatically protruding roofs and oblique curtain façades complete the deconstructivist ensemble.

'This store is unique, both to the Publix chain, and to Miami Beach, in that it incorporates an outdoor system of state of the art people and cart-mover ramps to bring shoppers and their purchases to the two levels of parking above the store. This innovative design solved the problem of parking, which is at a premium in Miami Beach. This system of exterior ramps also creates a strong visual statement for the store, carving out an attractive image and defining the corner of the two streets on which it is sited', says Wood and Zapata. The architects may not have been allowed any input as regards the interior of the box – the Publix teams will not relinquish control of the retail concept of their stores to anyone – but the avant-garde design of the exterior exercises sufficient pulling power to ensure that the tills ring out with even greater frequency. This eccentric superstore has achieved instant cult status, in a location which is hardly short of extravagant designs.

top: Front (above) and rear (below) elevations.

above: Plan of the whole site.

NO SKATEBOARDS
NO ROLLERBLADES
NO BICYCLES

NO CHILDREN IN SHOPPING
CARTS WHILE ON PEOPLE
MOVER

A steep, streamlined
staircase flanks the
wall of the supermar-
ket, while the gentler
slope of the moving
ramp takes the cus-
tomer with his or her
trolley back to the car
park via a scenic route.

opposite: View of the ramps descending from the upper parking levels to the ground floor; the shopper can take a break *en route* to look at the palm trees and view of the surrounding area.

above: The curving architecture of the façade set against the night sky provides Miami Beach with another extravagant landmark; the building enjoys a cult status within its locality.

Millennium Center

Budapest, Hungary, 1999
Interior Design: Mahmoudieh Design

Some people anticipated that with the end of the Communist regimes in Eastern Europe the old alliances would act as the vehicles of market liberalization, and that, for example, the old Austro-Hungarian Empire would provide at least an historical frame of reference for the economic turnaround in south-eastern Europe – but they were wrong. During the Cold War Vienna may have been regarded as a key inter-face for official (and indeed not-so-official) trade between East and West, but after 1990 Austria's companies and investors proved slow off the mark when it came to the opportunities opening up in the Czech Republic, Slovakia and Hungary. Since then they have managed to catch up – as is illustrated by projects like the Millennium Center in Budapest, which opened in 1999, developed by Austria's Girocredit bank.

The centre is housed in a prominent late-nineteenth-century listed building – with a well-preserved roof structure over its interior court-yard designed by legendary Parisian iron and glass architect Gustave Eiffel. It had been used as a market hall in the past and was therefore eminently suitable for the new mall planned for the site. This mall may not be exactly big, with around 7,000 square metres of useable floor space over three storeys, but it is all the more elegant for its relatively modest scale.

A total of US $35 million was invested in the conversion, the design of which was overseen and coordinated by German interior design company Mahmoudieh Design. In the words of company director Yasmine Mamoudieh, 'My aim was to provide a concept which allows and attracts movement from the exterior to within and throughout all floors of the interior,

above: Mahmoudieh Design's calm and elegant scheme for the interior of the former Budapest market hall was achieved by adopting a simple colour scheme throughout and ensuring that individual shop units were kept discreet and under-stated.

opposite: The fine nineteenth-century details of the Center, including an iron and glass roof by Gustave Eiffel, were retained, but the whole was en-livened by a cohesive lighting scheme which included a band of blue light running round the roofline and translu-cent slim light columns designed by Gerd Pfarré.

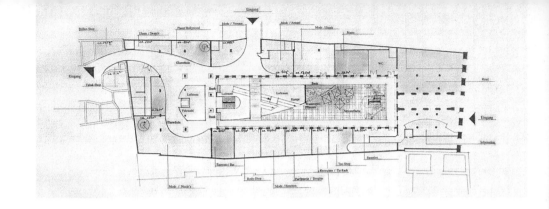

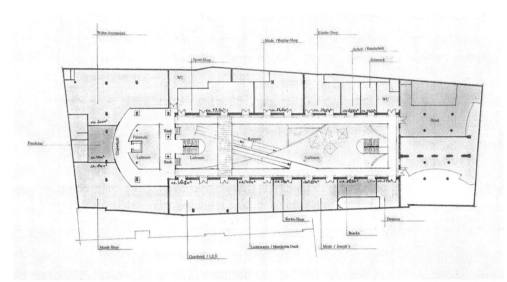

while maintaining a calm, quiet and harmonious appearance'. It is rare enough elsewhere, even in shopping centres of a higher architectural quality, for the individual tenants to be kept in line with the overall design. Here this conformity has been enforced, right through to the injunction that names and brands over shop entrances should be on sandblasted glass plaques uniformly lit with spotlights. Indeed the lighting scheme created by lighting designer Gerd Pfarré plays a central role throughout. A blue band of light frames the glass roof construction, and Pfarré has placed tall, slim, translucent column sculptures in the elongated atrium.

The Millennium Center is entered through three entrances with banners above, and instead of escalators, gently curved ramps lead in leisurely fashion from one storey to the next. In addition to retail outlets, the facilities include restaurants on the ground floor and office units on the top storey.

Plans of ground floor (top), first floor (centre) and basement (bottom).

The calm atmosphere of the atrium is enhanced by gentle ramps connecting the three floors, enabling customers to move about at a leisurely pace and encouraging them instinctively to ascend to the shops on the upper floors.

HEP FIVE

Osaka, Japan, 1998
Architecture: Takenaka Corporation

Shopping centre plus Ferris wheel equals mega-attraction: it was an obvious equation, but one that no-one had ever tried out in a city centre before. And it was in Japan of all places – so susceptible to earthquakes – that a huge piece of amusement-architecture was created to this formula. A thirty-year-old shopping centre in Kukata-cho, Kita-ku, at the heart of Osaka was demolished to make way for the new prodigy, the neighbouring plot of a former theatre was annexed, and the new Hankyu Entertainment Park – HEP FIVE, for short – was constructed.

'What we envisioned to do was to provide a fun shopping experience. The Ferris Wheel and retail space form a dynamic atmosphere and rhythm. The red Ferris Wheel built into the building is a symbol of the energy of city activity', said the architects of Takenaka Corporation who were responsible for this project. The completed project is a truly admirable feat of engineering. With a diameter of 75 metres, the fairground construction reaches its vertex at a dizzying 106 metres.

The design of HEP FIVE itself – which cost EUR 180 million and covers 52,755 square metres – is considerably less impressive. The six shopping storeys of the mall (plus two floors below ground level) offer a rather cheer-less spectacle; above the mall, the seventh floor houses the restaurant and the entrance to the big wheel, while the floor above this houses another function room. However, the monotony of the interior design did no harm at all in terms of the public response to the project, and the investors' most ambitious expectations were surpassed in dramatic fashion: in the first year of operation, nearly 20

above: The HEP FIVE shopping experience, in the heart of Osaka, takes place on six floors, lit by vast strip windows; the curving tail of a giant whale model adds life to the atrium.

opposite: The ingenious idea of constructing a giant Ferris wheel within the shopping centre has made the complex an overwhelming success; the 106-metre-high wheel itself is a huge feat of engineering.

million visitors flocked to the centre and 1.7 million of them went for a ride in the big wheel's 72 cabins. The pride of HEP's creators seems entirely reasonable in view of this popular acclaim: 'We believe that these numbers are the proof that we have established a new standard in the design and concept of an urban shopping centre. This is the entertainment-oriented urban shopping mall of the next Millennium,' said the Takenaka Corporation.

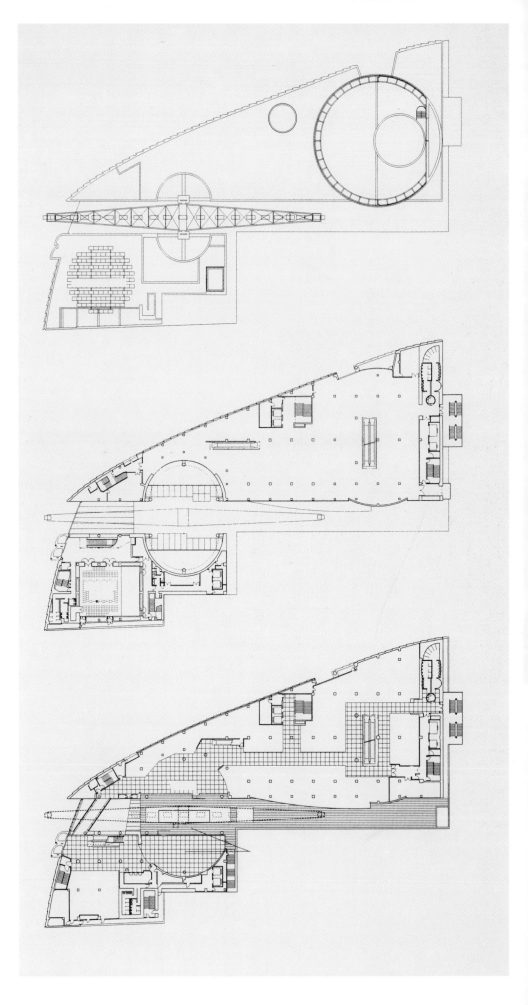

opposite top left: The escalators which criss-cross up and down the well of the central atrium are a dizzying sight from above.

opposite: Plans of two of the floors and the giant wheel in plan and laid flat.

The visitor is greeted at the entrance level of the atrium (there are two floors beneath ground level) by the striking red whale sculpture hanging in the central space which echoes the colour of the wheel.

The Forum Shops

Las Vegas, Nevada, USA, 1997
Architecture: Marnell Corrao Associates
Interior Design:
Dougall Design Associates

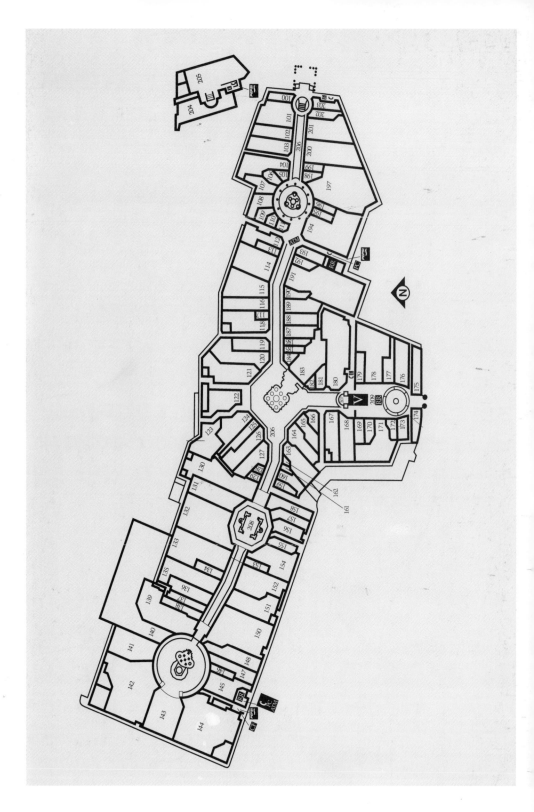

Everything in Las Vegas is designed to get people to part with their money. The city has risen to boomtown status thanks to its hugely popular gambling facilities and all the rest – shows, stars, entertainment – really serve only as highly enjoyable backdrops to sweeten the interludes between the roulette table and the gambling machines. This, at any rate, was for many years the conventional wisdom. The idea of building a top-class shopping mall on the bustling, glitzy strip was initially greeted by many with the scepticism it seemed to deserve. A space was available: a defunct racetrack was falling into decay right next-door to the mega-hotel Caesar's Palace. The investors supplied both the money and the experience: with more than 70 shopping centres in 20 American cities, the Simon Property Group is the leading owner, developer and operator in the sector in the USA. The theme was quickly decided, too: the plan was to create a piece of Ancient Rome next to the palace of the Caesars, providing a suitably imperial setting for exclusive brands such as Bulgari, Gucci and Armani and for popular shopping mall favourites such as Victoria's Secrets, F.A.O. Schwartz and Banana Republic.

When the first phase of the development opened and the crowds were thronging among the fake antiquities from morning through to late at night it quickly became clear that this was a goldmine: 'The Forum Shops' advanced in record time to become – measured by the square metre – the retail property with the highest turnover on the continent, indeed in the world. Since 1997 this neo-Roman tour de force has been resplendent in its completed

above: Plan of the complex which adjoins the Las Vegas land-mark Ceasar's Palace.

The Fountain of the Gods, offset by the changing moods of the artificially-lit 'sky', epitomises the flamboyance of the Las Vegas mall; the indoor lighting simulates the complete rhythm of daylight and night.

form, with a total floorspace of 47,000 square metres and more than 100 shops, cafés and restaurants. Its incredible pulling power is in large part due to the monumental setting created by Californian team Dougall Design Associates. The classical-style cityscape with temples, squares, fountains and mechanical gods that come to life on the hour is vaulted by an artificial firmament whose light changes as the day progresses. In the morning the sun rises, at midday the heavens are a bright mediterranean blue with delicate clouds, after this comes a pink sunset and at night there are twinkling stars. Terry Dougal says, 'The Forum Shops is entertainment. It transports the visitor into something totally unique.' The main attraction is 'Atlantis', where agile automated sculptures representing mighty gods and heroes eloquently dispute the fate of the legendary city, while iridescent tropical fish swim about mutely in a 250,000-litre marine aquarium. And there is more to look forward to: another 22,000 square metres will be added to this mini-Rome in the year 2002 – with a replica of the Pantheon as the centrepiece of the new district.

top: Douglas Design Associates created an entire firmament beneath the mall roof: one of the main routes as if lit by the Italian midday sun.

above: The replica ancient city abounds with decorative columns, balconies, dancing fountains and even a triumphal arch; pink hues capture the mood of an evening sunset.

A giant Trojan Horse keeps friendly watch over the entrance to a branch of the famous American toy shop chain F.A.O. Scwartz.

Europark

Salzburg, Austria, 1997
Architecture: Massimilano Fuksas

How fortunate for Salzburg, Austria's festival city, that its urban design advisory keeps a close eye on individual architectural projects. Had this public institution not existed then some soulless commercial confection would doubtless now be resplendent under the Europark banner on the motorway to Vienna. As it was, however, the committee organized an international competition which was won by none other than Rome-based avant-garde architect Massimiliano Fuksas. And he was at no loss for powerful words, even for this rather conventional commission: 'We immediately called it "breakpoint", after the title of a film which tells of a passion for surfing, of a man who tries to dominate nature, the great ocean waves; in other words, a passion for freedom'.

The wave idea alludes to the roofscape, nearly 300 metres long and made of red aluminium, with car parking facilities under it and the 40-metre high tapered structure of an aerial and viewing tower rising up out of it. And what about the sea? Arguably this is the blue-glazed, erratic-shaped box into which Fuksas has packed the mall's 150,000 square metres of useable floor space. His strategy is immediately apparent: these powerful symbols are intended to counteract the mundane fripperies of shops and brands. But even from the outside it is also clear that someone had to foot the bill for these grand ideas: the client, Austrian supermarket group Interspar, was allowed to advertise itself in storey-high characters that are just as prominent as the Europark sign.

Inside, the design has some successful and striking moments, with unusual daylight effects and exciting views up into the red roof structure,

above: Fuksas adopted the motif of a wave for one of Austria's largest shopping centres: the undulating red aluminium roof structure over the car park recalls the movement of the ocean; a 40-metre high viewing tower and aerial stands guard.

opposite: The centre announces its presence in storey-high, brightly illuminated letters; the main client, the supermarket Interspar, was afforded the same privilege.

but overall the conventional mix of commercial mediocrities prevails. 75 individual shops are grouped around five anchor stores, a Food Court and, more unusually, the studio of a local radio station, Club Radio Salzburg – the presenters broadcast their programmes live from a glass cabin in the upper storey.

With total construction costs of EUR 106 million, Salzburg's Europark is not the most expensive shopping centre in Austria, although it is one of the largest. The centre attracts an average of 10,000 visitors per day, including cross-border visitors from nearby Germany. And so Fuksas's huge wave has at least ful-filled the investors' commercial requirements by diverting the streams of shoppers that generally flow the other way over the border.

top: While the interior is a largely convention-al array of 75 individual shops and five anchor stores, the light which filters in from above provides a pleasant ambience.

above: Striking views of the red roof structure are available through the glass ceiling.

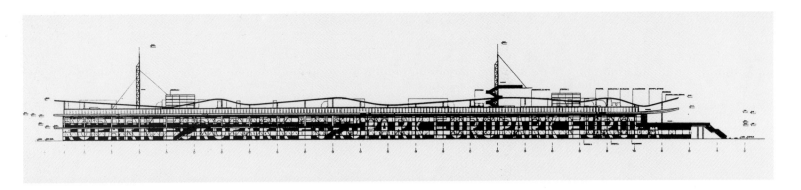

top: Elevation showing
the expanse of the
complex.

above: The rhythm of
the overhead structure
and the funnels which
add to the maritime
allusion create archi-
tectural incident to the
retail park, which is so
often a mundane
environment.

De Barones

Breda, The Netherlands, 1997
Architecture: CZWG Architects /
Kraaijvanger Urbis

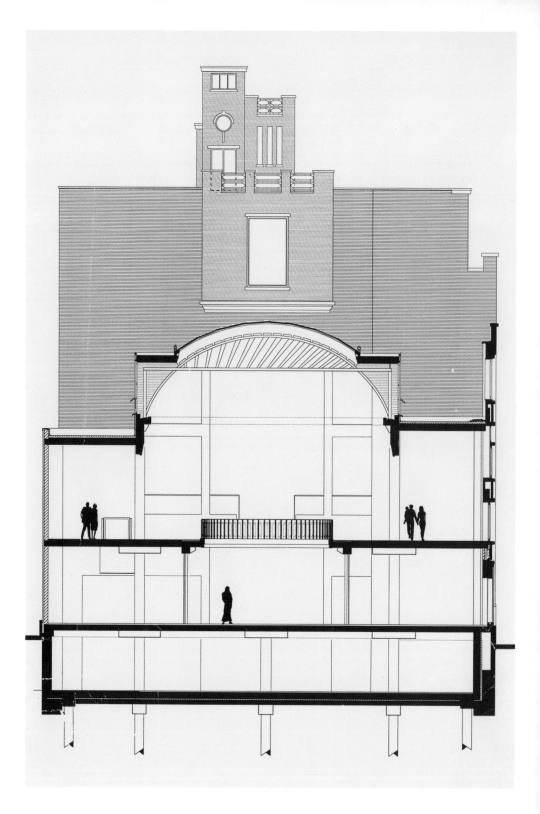

The task at De Barones was to carry out an urban renovation job in the historic centre of Breda. On the client side was an association of three different parties: the municipal authority, project developer MAB Groep and department store operator Vroom & Dreesmann, which occupied parts of the site. An independent committee, the 'Welstandscommisie', was specially set up to supervise the regeneration of the site, the restoration of listed buildings, and the demolition of some properties – as well as the monitoring the architectural and social quality of the project, planned as a mix of retail centre and residential units. Two architects' offices were given the commission: appointed alongside Dutch architects Kraaijvanger Urbis, who had experience of similar projects, was the successful London-based team CZWG (Nick Campbell, Rex Wilkinson and Piers Gough), famous for designs presenting variations on a theme of post-modern theatricality and witty bravura effects.

CZWG was responsible for the commercial part of the project: the De Barones shopping arcade, with 56 retail units covering 42,000 square metres of useable floor space. 'There is no simple solution to the problem of restructuring a large semi-derelict site in the heart of a medieval city centre and then stitching the whole seamlessly into the surrounding urban fabric. The design of the arterial shopping mall laces the multifarious elements of the scheme together: shopping centre, social and student housing and existing structures. Instead of an extended mall space, we designed a series of six linked "rooms", each with its own elegant roof of glazed steel trusses which filter the light,' said CZWG.

above: Section showing the main shopping levels and groupings.

opposite: The northern entrance to the centre is dominated by a decorative terracotta portcullis – a bold theatrical effect which has become something of a trademark for the complex.

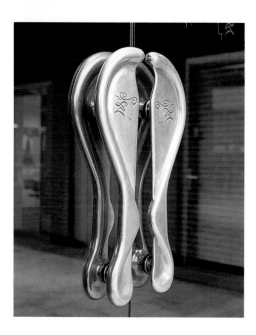

The two-storey architectural sequence of the De Barones centre, created with a budget in excess of EUR 38 million, presents an indoor street space, designed in an understated style and spanned by the light blue and brilliant white of the roof girders. One of the centre's major tenants is interior furnishings chain Habitat, which opened a branch in what was formerly a library. Over the north portal the architects set a monumental terracotta portcullis of ropes – a suggestive metaphor whose pronounced incongruity makes it a symbol for the reclamation of urban land. This decorative statement is not popular with the purists, but has effectively acquired the status of brand logo for this exemplary urban project, influential far beyond regional and national borders.

With the positive experience of Breda behind them, the CZWG team subsequently applied itself to another major project: the master plan for the ambitious Crown Street Regeneration Project in Glasgow, Scotland.

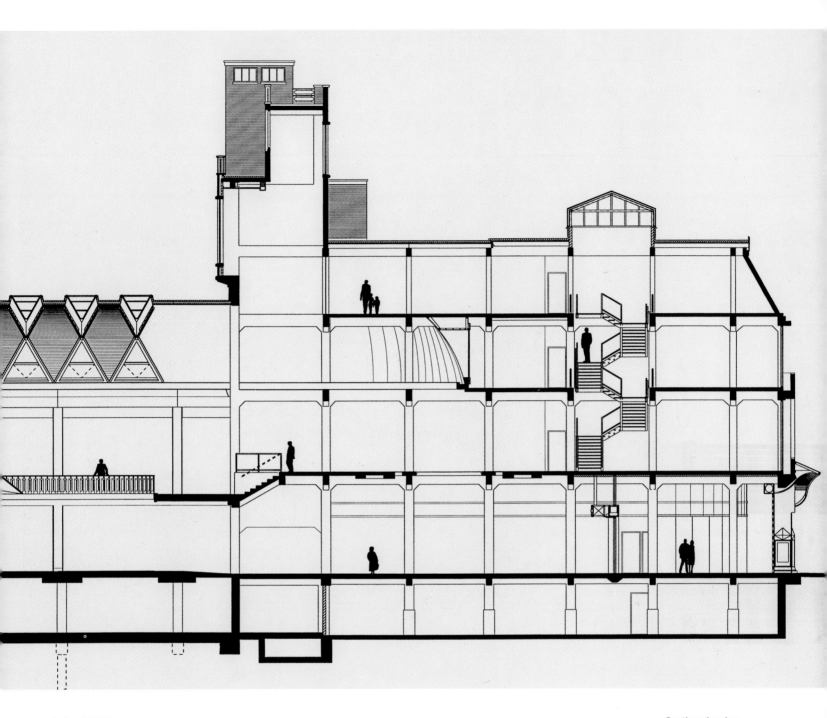

opposite top left: The
detailing of the centre
is highly wrought, as
these organically
shaped door handles
demonstrate.

opposite: The two-
storey interior is
elegantly lit and the
roof is constructed of
brilliant white girders
set off against a light
blue background.

Section showing
the staircases, roof
structure and service
areas.

Dick

Esslingen, Germany, 1998
Architecture: Heinz M. Springmann

Long-established Swabian firm Friedrich Dick still manufactures files and knives – no longer in its original location in the west of Esslingen, however, but in the outskirts where there is a steady proliferation of commercial buildings. Yet unlike many companies, who want nothing more to do with the legacy of the past, this metal products manufacturer involved itself, as investor and developer, in the rejuvenation of the large site, which occupies an entire block.

The company commissioned architect Heinz M. Springmann to create a lively arts, shopping and entertainment centre with a total useable floor space of 22,000 square metres from the industrial complex, whose oldest parts date from 1889. The project, completed within just 12 months at a cost of nearly EUR 31 million, is a remarkable success in both architectural and conceptual terms. The mix of functions and services extends beyond the conventional spectrum, and all the following coexist happily in the new 'Dick': a multiplex cinema with eight screens, shops and offices, a mega-disco with a capacity of 1,000, health and fitness studios, a variety of catering facilities, departments of the adult education institute and a mothers' centre. Everything was accommodated within the old buildings except for the newly built multi-storey car park.

The architect uses appropriate materials to create a kind of analogy to the industrial past. Rather than covering up the raw power of the original plant structures the massive relic dramatizes the historical construction effectively with colours and installations. The copious tangled piping and tubing of modern building technology meanders across walls and under the ceilings.

above: The firm of Friedrich Dick decided to get involved in the rejuvenation of its former massive industrial premises; the new commercial initiative did not abandon the structural relics of the past, such as the original roof girders.

opposite: A highly original and diverse mix of activities is housed in the complex: a diving pool in the main hall intersects two storeys and allows scuba divers to practise their skills in front of an audience.

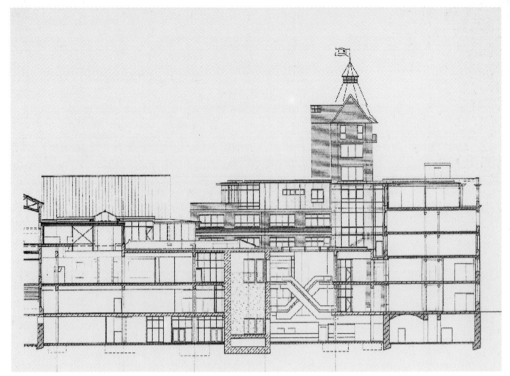

The diving pool intersecting two storeys in the main hall offers an unconventional spectacle for visitors to the centre, who can watch divers perfecting their marine skills through its windows. Four new entrances lead into the entertainment and shopping centre; inside, thematically arranged shopping arcades lead off from a central piazza.

In commercial terms 'Dick' is certainly a success, if not unreservedly so. The cinemas and discos attract a noisy, youthful clientèle, but so far the retail operations have not really got off the ground: one year after the centre opened, more than half of the shopping space was still unoccupied. The developer and the city authorities are still debating whether this is exclusively attributable to Germany's restrictive store-opening hours – at night, when crowds are flocking to the cinemas and dance floors, the shops have to close by 8p.m. – or to poor travel connections with the city centre. It may be that there is still some fine-tuning to be done on the project's concept and marketing strategy, to add the necessary final touches to this historic company's excursion into the property development business.

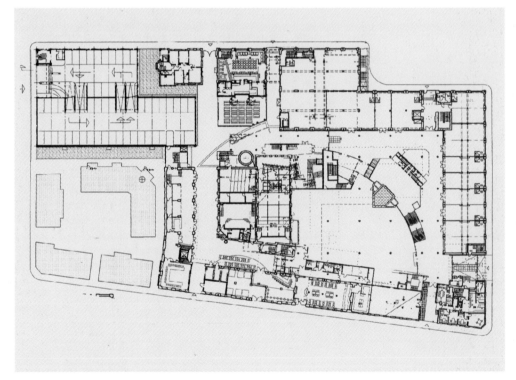

top left: A rock climber scales the wall/artificial mountain surface with his back to the escalators and enormous airy space of the centre.

top: Section showing the complexity and size of the complex.

above: Plan

The metal piping and ducts which form a network over the entire structure, as well as the industrial size lamps suspended from great heights, pay homage to the building's industrial past.

Chelsea Market

New York, New York, USA, 1997
Architecture: Jeff Vandeberg

Biscuit-lovers the world over will be familiar with the products of American food multinational Nabisco. When this group was still called National Biscuit Company, it made its products on west Manhattan's 10th Avenue, on a factory site comprising 18 buildings constructed between 1890 and 1940. After the site was abandoned, the property passed into the hands of an investor who chose an unconventional option: instead of simply flattening the defunct industrial buildings he gave architect Jeff Vandeberg plenty of time to come up with a new use for the site, proceeding with sensitivity and care.

The process of transformation lasted four years and began in experimental fashion. The architect worked his way forward without a definitive master plan, laying bare the spatial qualities of the existing structures as though he were undertaking an archaeological excavation. 'There was a great deal we didn't know about in the interior of the buildings. There were a lot of workshops and rooms, but we couldn't see the wood for the trees. First of all we had to pull down or move the existing fittings and internal constructions in order to give the building a new cohesion,' Vandeberg stated.

A lively city-centre bazaar of varied small shops is housed in the former Nabisco factory site which architect Jeff Vandeberg, in an archaeological approach to the project, discovered was originally designed to house freight trains.

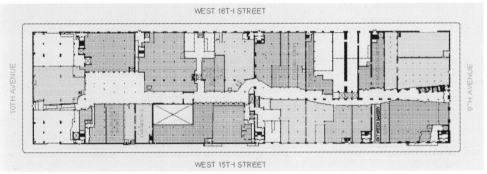

The largest shed construction, originally designed for freight trains, forms the new, 243 metre-long central axis of Chelsea Market. A lively mix of vegetable shops, bakers', fishmongers, delicatessens, cafés and much more besides transforms the rough, unadorned factory architecture, covering 15,000 square metres, into an attractive city-centre bazaar.

Instead of cutting cleanly and neatly through the surrounding brick walls, ruined Gothic portals enact a brutal surgery into the past. A striking feature of this interventionist strategy is the complete absence of that rose-tinted nostalgia so often encountered in regeneration projects of this type. Here there is no kitsch take on the past, no ornate, pseudo-historical ambience. Vandeberg took the opposite path, creating – in collaboration with artist Mark Mennin – a theme tour of objects and installations leading through the entire ground floor of the former factory site. Rough granite pillars flank passageways, relief sculptures in stone and metal hang on the walls, fluted slabs of rock surround a water pipe which rises up from a gaping hole in the wall, constantly pumping up water which flows back down into a deep well.

Yet the brilliantly conceived Chelsea Market is not all there is to this renovation project. In the upper storeys of the old biscuit factory, too, the past has moved out and the future has moved in – with film studios, production companies, internet operators and the full panoply of multimedia services.

top: Vandeberg collaborated with artist Mark Mennin to create a series of installations on the ground floor of the building, such as this crude waterfall protruding from a gaping hole in the wall.

above : Plan of the Market, situated between 9th and 10th Avenues and West 15th and 16th Streets.

The approach to regeneration was decidedly un-nostalgic and occasionally rough: gothic portals were rudely ripped out of the brick walls with stunning effect.

Promenaden Hauptbahnhof

Leipzig, Germany, 1997
Architecture: ECE Projektmanagement

At its ceremonial opening in 1915 this was the world's largest railway terminus, boasting a façade that was 300 metres long and two of everything. The royal Prussian and Saxon railways had joined forces to bestow this splendid specimen of railway architecture on the city of Leipzig, dividing it with the utmost care and federal exactitude right down the middle. And so there were two identical entrance halls, two waiting rooms exactly the same size, two stationmaster's offices, and so on. All that is history now: the intervening years have seen two wars, two German dictatorships and any number of misdeeds. Rather battered, but with its dignity intact, the railway station withstood the tests of time, and after German reunification it underwent a renaissance which once again broke all the records: when it was re-opened in 1997 after an express modernization which took just two years to complete, it was not only the world's largest railway-linked shopping centre, but also one of the most expensive railway renovation projects, representing a total investment of EUR 256 million.

Since then this monumental edifice has been trading under the brilliant 'Promenaden' logo: along an airwell set deep into the seemingly endless hall that runs along the platform ends there are 120 shops, plus 18 cafés and bistros, accommodated over two floors and 30,000 square metres. Reunification also brought the two German railway companies together and for the reunified Deutsche Bahn this Leipzig showpiece was the pilot project in a new image-restoring initiative, 'Renaissance of the railway stations' (the title of an exhibition proudly displayed at the architecture Biennale in Venice), designed to transform its run-down

above: The renovation of the Leipzig station was a sympathetic yet forward-looking modernization, with glass high-tech lifts referring to the proliferation of glass used on the original platform roofs.

opposite: The sumptuousness of old Prussia was revived, albeit with up-to-date furnishings, so that travellers can once again sit under the beautifully coffered waiting room ceilings.

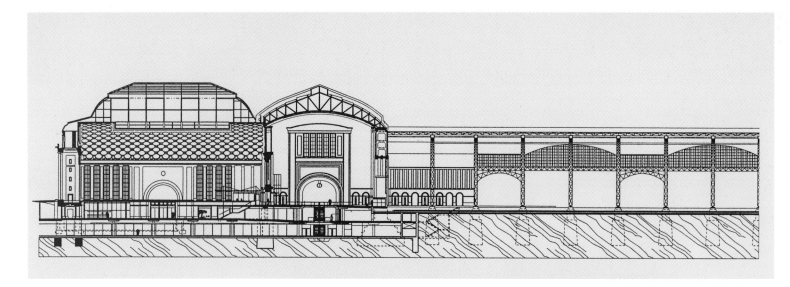

passenger terminals into attractive, customer-friendly service centres that can stand up to comparison with today's airports. But even the railway company's modernization budget – estimated at more than EUR 10 billion in all – was not sufficient to bring off the Leipzig transformation. The lion's share of the necessary funding was raised by a closed-end property fund set up by Europe's biggest mall operator, ECE of Hamburg, and Deutsche Bank. That this vast sum of money was wisely invested is apparent not so much from the conventional design of the 'Promenaden' as from the historical substance of this venerable colossus. It is an astonishing experience to walk through these painstakingly restored and beautifully renovated halls.

Travellers can once again while away the time between trains in the proper style and comfort, in the old Prussian waiting room with its long bar. The former Saxon waiting room is regularly used for concerts and other public events. Here in Leipzig, diners can rediscover the lost splendour of railway restaurants, sitting under the high, colourful coffered ceilings. Even the opulent stationmaster's rooms have been allocated an appropriate use, providing a magnificent setting for small conferences, business lunches or private parties.

top: Transverse section

above: The huge central section of the station provided capacity for 120 shops and 18 eateries, creating a shopping environment for travellers to rival any modern airport.

The station was the world's largest terminus when it opened in 1915; with German reunification it underwent a transformation (taking a mere two years to complete) creating the world's largest railway-linked retail outlet.

opposite: The stone-work of the original halls has been impressively renovated and the clean lines of the contemporary additional structures and signage are satisfyingly unobtrusive.

above: The hall which runs along the side of the platforms is seemingly endless – a brilliantly lit, customer-friendly service centre that marks a new renaissance for the railway station.

Munich Airport Center

Munich, Germany, 1999
Architecture: Murphy/Jahn

When the city of Munich moved its international airport to the open wastelands of the Erdinger Moos district in the early 1990s, the intention was to design an airport in as uninvasive a way possible. The kilometre-long white terminal building was deliberately built at a low level, and its contours were often obscured from view in the misty air in the moorland setting. However, restraint has become a thing of the past since Helmut Jahn, a US architect of German origin, started making his dramatic mark on the airport site. The latest example of this is the Munich Airport Center (MAC), a multifunctional ensemble including a shopping mall, catering facilities, offices, a conference area and a plaza (called the Forum), covered over by a fibreglass membrane that is 90 metres wide and 41 metres high. Jahn's neighbouring high-tech hangar from 1994, which houses the Kempinski Hotel, looks positively unassuming by comparison.

This is the ideal location for observing the evolutionary process by which airports are steadily mutating into department stores with a landing strip attached. With nearly 40 shops and showrooms, the MAC is far more than just a utility wing designed to meet the basic needs of arriving and departing travellers. Especially as Jahn has deliberately designed the

Helmut Jahn's dramatic roof over the multifunctional MAC complex is a fibreglass membrane stretching over 90 metres at a height of 41 metres; the huge centre includes Audi car showrooms.

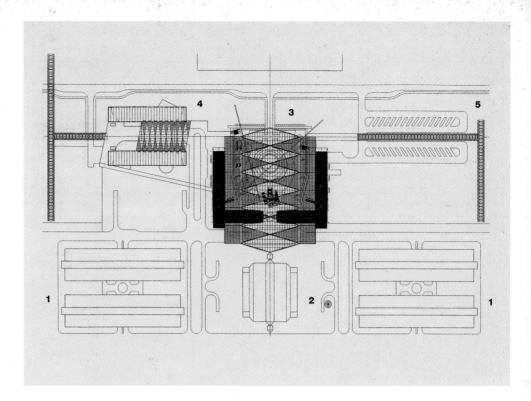

six-storey complex, with its two L-shaped wings and extravagant roof construction as the 'heart' of the site intended to stand out from afar as the 'centrepoint of the total urban concept and visible symbol'.

The MAC has a total of 31,000 square metres of usable floorspace. On the entrance level it offers customers a range of facilities including a supermarket, fashion stores, a shoe shop, a jeweller's, a tea shop, multimedia retailers, and a variety of catering outlets – including a good-sized Bavarian pub with its own built-in microbrewery – as well as impressive showrooms for car manufacturers Audi and Lamborghini. Above this there are medical and legal practices, office service providers hiring out fully-equipped temporary offices, the Municon conference centre and the German head office of a sanitary paper products manufacturer. In commercial terms it would seem that the MAC has fulfilled the expectations of its investors, who pumped a total of EUR 123 million into the ambitious project: by the time the building opened in October 1999, 70 per cent of the floor space had been let at city-centre rates. The prospects for the future look even rosier: a second airport terminal is scheduled to open in 2003, raising passenger numbers from the current 20 million to 35 million per year.

top: Site plan
1 car parking
2 West Terminal
3 MAC
4 Kelpinski Hotel
5 bus terminal

above: The six-storey wings of the centre form two L-shapes, and provide 31,000 square metres of useable floorspace.

Between the masts the main steel beams run diagonally. The glazed sections between the diamond-shaped membranes consist of clear laminated glass with a substructure of steel pipe, trusses and tension rods.

chapter four the great comeback

The changing face of department stores

The old shopping havens that have been pronounced dead are refusing to give up the ghost, or returning to life in a new guise. Many marketing experts held out little hope for the future of the traditional department stores. After nearly one and a half centuries of success, fame and honour, the proud 'cathedrals of modern trade' celebrated by Emile Zola seemed to be facing an apparently inexorable decline. Too big, too ponderous and too unselective, went the verdict. With the exception of a few stores in top locations the outlook was bleak for these dinosaurs: the new discount stores were attracting more customers, cut-price cash and carry outlets in the urban peripheries were eroding their margins, and their wide, unfocused ranges were proving to be an Achilles heel. Yet cometh the time and cometh the solution, as everyone knows. Strategists at a number of department store chains saw the crisis as an opportunity for repositioning and refocusing. Established stores were rejuvenated with new, more targeted consumer concepts, and new greenfield stores were developed with entrepreneurial imaginativeness. Where impressive shopping centres and mega-malls want to pull in the crowds and where hundreds of individual retail units are grouped together, the quality of the major department store names is a crucial ingredient for success, acting as a magnet for consumers. This is the 'anchor store' role, tried and tested over decades in the USA, and now also proving an effective vehicle for the comeback of today's slimmed-down, rejuvenated department stores in Europe and Asia.

Lust for Life

Aachen, Germany, 1999
Architecture: Kister Scheithauer Gross
Interior Design: Umdasch Shop-Concept

The crisis of the traditional department store chains has the same causes everywhere, but not the same effects. The poorly-defined, middle-of-the-road ranges offered by city-centre department stores are finding it hard to compete with more finely-tuned retail concepts and with the new retail parks on the urban peripheries, which are attracting droves of car-driving shoppers to their clusters of discount stores and malls. As a result, store closures are frequent, and the process of concentrating on a few sites in prime locations is gathering pace.

However, Germany's Kaufhof group shows that things can be different, and that determinedly focusing on individual customer groups can offer an alternative to closing down. Once Kaufhof's slogan, typically, offered its customers 'everything under one roof'; the group's current strategy, by contrast, is based on clear segmentation – the 'Emotions' branch concept is aimed at appealing to contemporary women, 'Lust for Life' is designed for younger, trend-conscious consumers.

The pilot project for the 'Lust for Life' concept is the conversion of a former Kaufhof store at the heart of Aachen, on the western German border. Cologne-based architects Kister Scheithauer Gross decided to signal the store's redefinition with a radical intervention in the façade of the building. They cut two large, coloured circular openings into the timeworn

Spots and large pendant factory-type lights combine with square metal display stands to create a theatrical, loft-like environment.

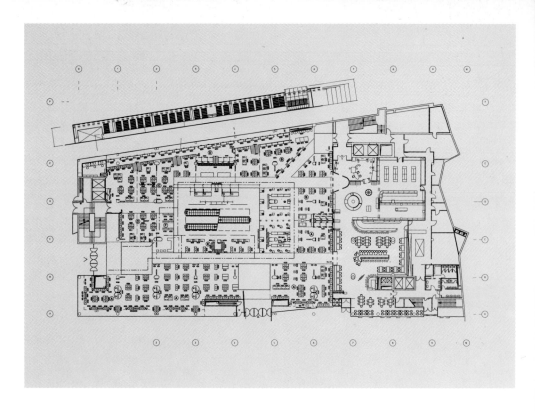

honeycomb curtain façade from the 1970s, removed the inner screens of the glass front behind it and also got rid of all the false ceilings and most of the partition walls from the sales floors. 'The curtain of prefabricated concrete becomes a membrane revealing new and totally surprising perspectives from both inside and outside. Opening up the building is the central theme – for example, cutting into the virtual passageways which operate like the streets of an urban block. These two primary measures enabled us to preserve the identity of the building and at the same time restructure the space as a whole, within a limited budget,' said Kister Scheithauer Gross.

The hermetic structure of the old department store is indeed opened up and, inside, the musty 1970s atmosphere has been replaced by the loft-style ambience of an imaginatively converted industrial building. The high ceilings have been left bare, exposing the building's pipes and wires. The display systems and the square metal frames of the retail furniture create the effect of a temporary stage set. The silver shades of the massive pendant lights, along with simple theatrical spotlights, further underpin the studio-style, industrial feel of the whole.

top: Ground floor plan

above: Architect's sketch of the circular intrusions into the 1970s façade of the building.

opposite: The bulk of the sales floor partition walls were removed and those that stayed were painted white or rust-red; false ceilings were also stripped away to leave pipework visible – intriguing new vistas were opened up in the process.

opposite: The retail space is a successful fusion of industrial and studio aesthetics – a relaxed feel is further suggested with occasional chairs, coffee table and a rug on the stripped wooden floor positioned in front of the red window arch.

above: The restaurant area continues the modern, informal tone of the store, with tables and benches in different styles; a tiered wine-bottle chandelier above the entrance provides a playful touch.

Bloomingdales Aventura

Miami, Florida, USA, 1997
Architecture: Kevin Kennon,
Kohn Pedersen Fox Associates
Interior Design:
Robert Young Associates

The Aventura Mall in north Miami is not a new
shopping destination, but since its latest
extension, designed by New York architects
Kohn Pedersen Fox Associates, opened in
November 1997 it has gained an additional
architectural attraction. For the client, American
department store chain Bloomingdales, this
project represented an important step towards
a new branch store concept: 'The intention is
to move away from the "blank box" of traditional department stores and allow the activities,
color, image and merchandise to interact with
the outside in dynamic and interactive ways,'
explains Kevin Kennon, the architect responsible for the project. However, the pursuit of
transparency and innovative architectural
methods had to take account of the con-
straints of commerce at the same time.

In Florida the key issues were to cut out the
omnipresent nuisance of dazzling sunlight, with
its high UV levels, and at the same time to
ward off the dangers posed by hurricanes,
which are by no means a rarity in this region.
The architects therefore focused their energies
primarily on the costly façade construction. On
the west front and the southern corner of the
building this consists of transparent, translucent and opaque glass panels covered on the
outside with sheets of perforated steel. This

**Kohn Pedersen Fox
made virtue out of ne-
cessity with the land-
mark façade which,
with opaque glass
panels and perforated
steel sheets, stands up
to the threats of hurri-
canes and sunlight.**

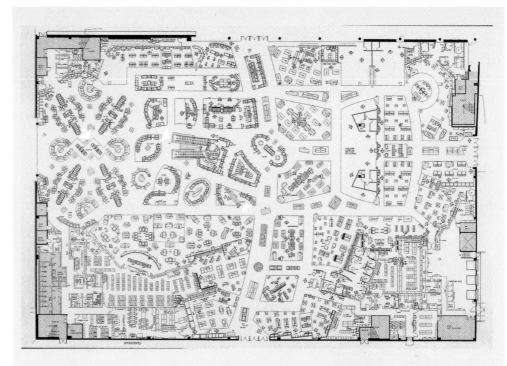

dual membrane effectively screens the sunlight while the metal cladding is designed to prevent the danger of high winds breaking the glass. The motifs of this double curtain façade are echoed in the pattern of the walls, in the decorative overhanging ledges and metal cladding. Above the main entrance, on the car-park side, the architects set a large square screen, which displays projected up-to-date customer information and advertising during the evening and at night.

Bloomingdales entrusted old hands Robert Young Associates with the interior design, covering a total of 23,300 square metres of useable floorspace. This company, based in Dallas, Texas, is one of the USA's leading retail design specialists and has for many years taken care of all significant renovation and construction projects undertaken by the Bloomingdales Group. It is indicative of their painstaking professionalism that the interior decor and furnishings of the Aventura branch have been designed to match the unconventional architecture of the building, underpinning its efforts to replace the hermetic concrete box formula with an effect of transparency and light.

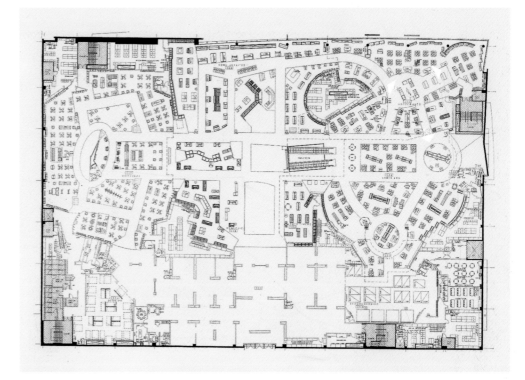

top left: The light, informal and open interior design by Robert Young Associates, is in keeping with the exterior.

above: Ground (bottom) and first floor (top) plans showing the interior store layout

The café area, situated behind the opaque glass panels is bright and airy, yet not overwhelmed by the Florida sunshine; chequerboard tables pick up on a motif used on the floor elsewhere in the interior.

opposite: A curving
bank of white televi-
sion monitors, which
blend in with the clean
ceilings and walls, are
a novel twist on in-
store security systems.

above: a large white
screen above the west
entrance forms an in-
trinsic element of the
horizontals and verti-
cals façade pattern and
is used in the evenings
to project customer in-
formation and promo-
tions to those in the
car park.

Warenhuis Vanderveen

Assen, The Netherlands, 1998
Architecture: Herman Hertzberger

At 68, Herman Hertzberger is the grand old man of contemporary Dutch architecture, with the status of moral guru as well as architectural master. His designs are concerned with social usefulness rather than display. According to Hertzberger, cultural value does not reside in the architecture itself: all that matters is how well it functions as a (more or less) public space, as an object that is used and experienced on a day-to-day basis. All of which may not be especially popular in times when architecture is viewed primarily as a marketing tool and as such made subservient to commercial or regional interests.

But Hertzberger's philosophy is in no way disproved by the current dominance of artist-architects. A relatively small project, the annexe of a provincial department store in Assen in the Netherlands, shows how successful a synthesis of architectural impact and urban re-definition can be. Over the previous decades, Assen's department store Warenhuis Vanderveen had slowly and steadily expanded to spread over an entire block, with haphazard additions across a patchwork of plots. As a result of some skillful negotiation, the company obtained permission to move the building line bordering a public square forwards by six metres, across the full length of the building.

Herman Hertzberger created maximum impact and brought a flavour of the big city to a public square in provincial Assen by attaching an all-glass annexe to the existing store façade.

The commission for the annexe was given to Hertzberger, who opted for a radical and striking solution: 'We thought that here, in a provincial town where people are more accustomed to largely closed brick facades, an almost entirely glass construction – the strongest possible contrast – would be capable of adding to the ambience of a big city'.

Instead of taking up all the available space, the annexe is placed in front of the existing façade like a satellite, an autonomous longitudinal body towering above the existing eaves. The one-and-a-half metre gap this creates is spanned by footbridges. The transparency of the annexe which is 'positioned in front of the existing block like a ship at moorings' (Hertzberger) becomes more pronounced towards the top of the building: from the appropriately named Koopmansplein (merchants' square) the sky is visible through the top storey. The maritime metaphor used by Hertzberger does not sufficiently express the benefit in quality that Assen's town centre has gained from the Vanderveen extension. The slim glass block gives the square a new and sharper contour. At the same time it is no coincidence that the structure of the façade is reminiscent of the department store buildings of the 1960s, which have since acquired such a terrible reputation. This is perhaps the irony of the project: many an architect would have been tempted to complete Assen's department store with pseudo-historical camouflage; Hertzberger, by contrast, reminds us of yesterday's stylistic models, and shows us how, with a few decisive shifts of emphasis, they can still contribute to a positive urban experience.

above left: The annexe gives its surroundings a new contour, and its canopy and materials are in marked contrast to the brick buildings of the town.

above: Section view of the annexe attached to the existing building.

above left and above:
'Gangplanks' link the
existing building to the
annexe, crossing a
1.5-metre-deep atrium
which rises the full
height of the building .

Emporium

Bangkok, Thailand, 1997
Architecture/Interior Design:
Jacqueline & Henri Boiffils

Thailand's capital has still not recovered from the financial crisis in Asia of the late 1990s. The decaying concrete structures of speculative office blocks tower up into the sky above Bangkok, and many shopping centres stand desolate and empty. When plans got under way for the Emporium, which opened in 1997, no-one could have foreseen that the boom times – with double-digit growth rates and quick riches for everyone, not just the business elite – would come to such an abrupt end.

The local investor at the head of one of the country's largest trading companies wanted to create an exceptional venue for luxury and fashion the like of which had never been seen before in Bangkok or the other major cities of the region. Her search for interior designers for this top assignment took her to the other side of the globe, where she identified candidates in Italy, the UK and France. Her final choice showed that her instincts were sound: Paris-based team Jacqueline & Henri Boifills operate, in the best sense, in the grand tradition of French retail stage-setting, the décor of mercantile seduction whose beginnings were so impressively described by Emile Zola in his novel *Au Bonheur des Dames* at the end of the nineteenth century. Just as in those days the Parisian paradigm became established as the norm, a blueprint that conquered all the world's leading cities, so the contemporary version created by the Boifills in copybook projects for top clients such as Le Printemps was now to be exported from the Seine to the Prao.

The concept of a high-quality department store set amidst shopping arcades was an excellent basis for the design, ensuring that the overall effect was not dependent on the public

above: Each floor in the store is distinguished by its own colourful and ornamental elements: in the shoe department, display boxes jutting from a pillar, urn-like stools and a pattern of coloured dots on the floor add playful touches – the Boiffils took 17th- and 18th-century French gardens as their inspiration.

opposite: Circular, balconied stairwells on three sides of the building lead up through six floors; the neutral colour scheme allows each department to make its own statement more easily.

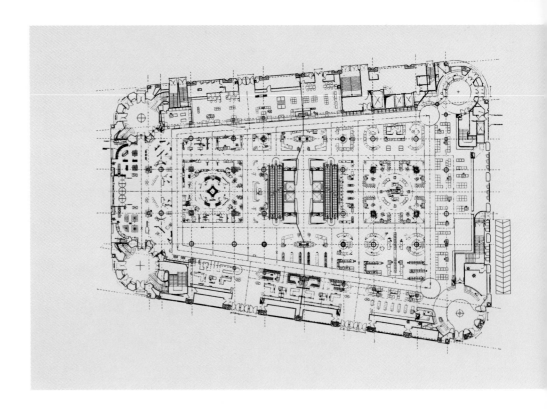

spaces, as usual, but focused on the six storeys of the department store. The quantum leap in terms of quality is clear: instead of the 'same Hollywood-type sort of cardboard architecture' that is the norm in glitzy malls from Hong Kong to Singapore, the Paris team was seeking to create 'the equivalent of something made to measure, the concept of luxury and its architectural expression, the very opposite of the ephemeral'. Every different floor in the department store tells its own subtle story of colours, ornaments and materials, within which the displays of merchandise are arranged with an elegant lightness of touch. The love of detail borders on the playful, adding up to an overall light-heartedness of effect which makes the Emporium a high point in the contemporary department store revival.

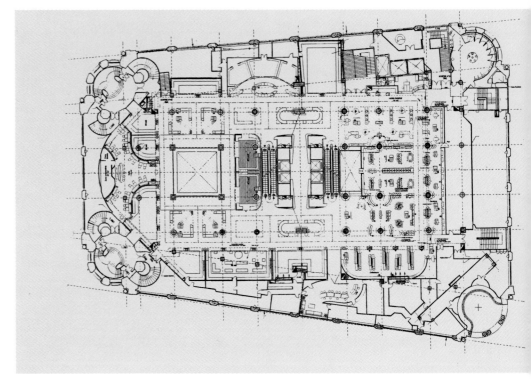

top: Ground floor plan

above: First floor plan

above top: Bold striped seating material and outsize photographs are used effectively in a café area situated on the top floor – unusual for this type of store in Asia where restaurants are often relegated to the basement.

above centre: Multicoloured lanterns are hung at different levels to create interest in the stairwells.

above: Light-hearted decoration in the lingerie department is elegantly achieved – contemporary shapes and materials act as metaphors for natural elements such as leaves.

above: The aim behind the project was to create an elegant and luxurious retail destination; this was carried out with a lightness of touch and rich and inventive interior detailing.

Georges

Melbourne, Australia, 1998
Architecture: Daryl Jackson Architects
Interior Design: Daryl Jackson Interiors /
Conran Design Partnership

above: The space was
enhanced by new
transparent tinted
glass display stands
set onto a neutrally
coloured polished floor.

When the Georges department store opened
on Melbourne's Collins Street in 1880, the
Australian metropolis finally had a pièce de
résistance that could bear comparison with the
newly-fashionable consumer temples in
Europe's great cities. Yet just like its models,
after decades of prosperity Georges fell upon
hard times. By the end of the twentieth
century, new retail concepts, lost customers
and an outdated merchandise mix were
increasingly making the generalist approach to
retailing an anachronism. And like department
stores elsewhere in the world, this Melbourne
institution had to prescribe itself a radical cure
in order to survive.

As well as taking the customary remedies –
focusing on fashion, beauty, gourmet foods
and home accessories – the store sought
salvation from a design-led renovation of the
building and by creating a range of fashionable
catering facilities. For the Melbourne team of
architects which was entrusted with the renovation, this was a project of great local and
patriotic significance, as company boss Daryl
Jackson emphasizes: 'Memory and prospect
are brought together in the new Georges.
Former customers will recall the past; a new
generation with another sense of style can use
their imagination, as we all move into another
future. There is a transforming idea here that
Melbourne has always expressed and thought
to be necessary.'

The team's aim was to uncover the historic
fabric, enhance it and fill it with new contents.
The first step was the restoration of the historic
atrium and the original grid of pillars covering
the entire elongated floorplan of the building.
To support this new authenticity, the floors in

The historic atrium of the venerable department store was rediscovered in the refurbishment programme, and a gleaming new staircase and glass balconies were inserted into the fabric.

the upper storeys were laid with patinated wood flooring, cut from the original beams of a demolished wool warehouse in Adelaide.

For the interiors, reinforcements were brought in from London: not only did the practised teams of the Conran Design Partnership help fit out the sales and restaurant areas, but Sir Terence Conran also established his first Australian Conran Shop in the new Georges. Furthermore, he even allowed the head chef of Quaglinos, his successful London restaurant, to be lured away to provide suitably high-class fare for diners down under in the loft bistro The Canteen, in the basement Brasserie and in the Café by the street.

When the doors of the revitalized Georges – achieved at a cost of AU $25 million – opened in February 1998, the staff, dressed in chic black designer outfits, were ready to greet the hordes of consumers the project was intended to attract. And indeed at first sheer curiosity did bring the masses through the doors – but purchasers of the upmarket merchandise remained few and far between. Barely two years after the official opening the new Georges there were rumours of closure. Perhaps this facelift was too upmarket to make a profit?

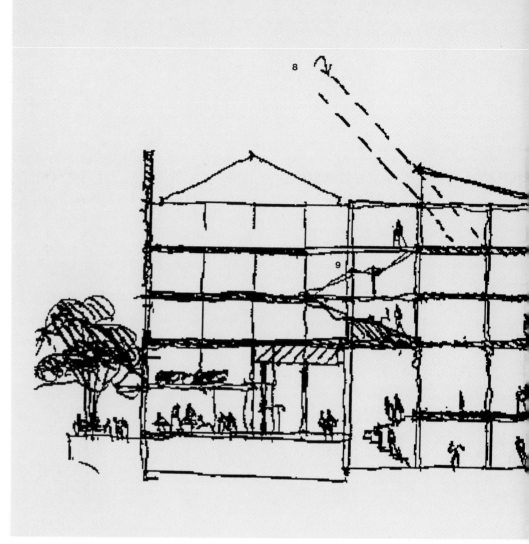

top left: Patinated wood flooring on the upper levels was made from the original beams of an old Adelaide warehouse.

top: Sketch section
1 lower level restaurant
2 accessories level
3 fashion level
4 living/home level
5 studio/loft/gallery
6 glass roof light
7 glass floor
8 south light
9 new stair

above: The glass balconies enhance the feeling of light within.

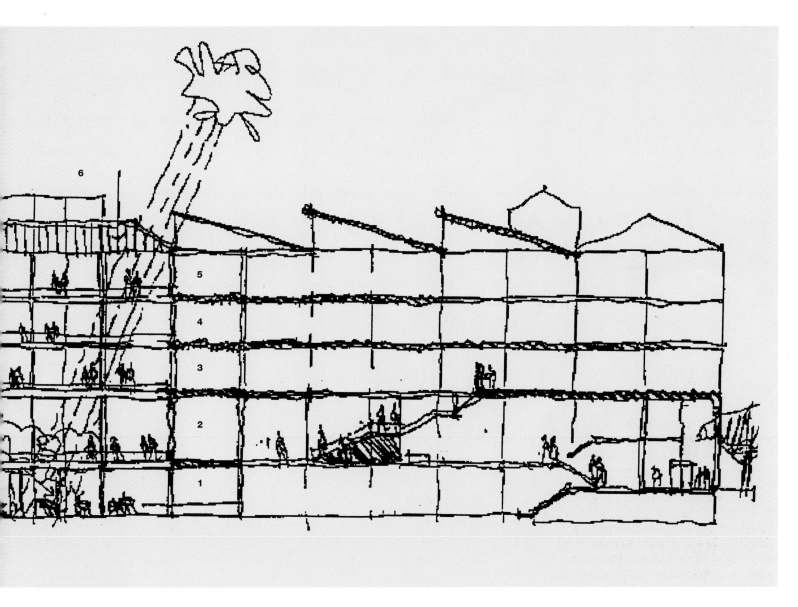

6

5

4

3

2

1

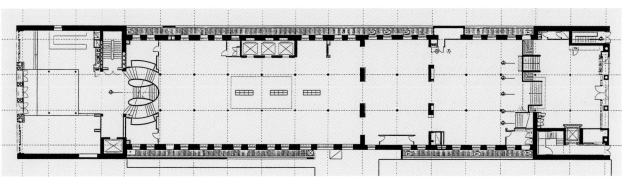

above: Ground floor plan

Selfridges Trafford Centre

Manchester, UK, 1998
Architecture: Chapman Taylor Partners
Interior Design:
John Herbert Partnership /
Conran Design Partnership /
Gerard Taylor, Aldo Cibic

If a postcard of this fantasy mall were to fall through the letterbox without any postmark, the recipient might guess that it had come from Las Vegas or Dubai – they would be unlikely to guess that this was Manchester. And yet this phantasmagorical mix of classical architecture, Arabian nights, Versailles and St Peter's is indeed located in the prosperous suburbs of this British city which has been renovating itself rapidly in recent years.

The mall is called The Trafford Centre, has a vast useable floorspace and cost the impressive sum of EUR 920 million to build. This postmodern consumer stage-set was conjured up by the architects of British company Chapman Taylor Partners, who have achieved success with shopping centres and other major projects across the globe.

There would have been no point at all in Selfridges, an historic company founded in 1909, trying to replicate the decorative splendours of its famous London department store so it wisely opted for an alternative strategy in its first venture outside the capital. It was lured to the Trafford Centre with the promise of an undisputed leading role in its creation: as the anchor store, built over two storeys and covering 18,600 square metres. The John Herbert Partnership, appointed by Selfridges as interior

The glass-domed exterior of the Selfridges department store, with hints of Versailles, gives some indication of the grandness of scale at the Trafford Centre; Selfridges is the anchor store of the mega-mall.

designers, took a bold approach to the project and 'used this opportunity to create a modern contemporary store marking the next generation of Selfridges' retail commitment'. Bringing other designers on board was part of the concept from the outset: 'A department store is characterized by its multiple personalities and so it is very logical to employ more than one design viewpoint in creating a retail theatre,' they said.

As well as coming up with the shop's overall design concept, John Herbert Partnership took on three of the five main areas: Spirit (the fashion mecca), Men's Contemporary (the men's department) and the Beauty Hall. The Conran Design Partnership applied itself to creating the Spirit Café, while British-Italian duo Gerard Taylor and Aldo Cibic were brought in to design the Food Hall. The diverse individual styles are united by a shared belief in a pared-down style and a love of carefully-considered detail. The only, probably unavoidable, concessions to the over-the-top glitz of the mega-mall – even the toilet entrances are presented as Egyptian temple façades – are the red marble frieze above the main entrance and the golden dome over the Beauty Hall. These are the only visible signs that even sober elegance has its price: Selfridges's Manchester excursion cost no less than EUR 30.7 million.

top: The interior design of the 'clublike' Spirit fashion department – aimed at young people – on level two, by John Herbert Partnership, is reached by an organically-shaped double staircase in moleanos limestone with carefully detailed balustrade, the shape of which is echoed in the skylight above.

above: The Women's Contemporary clothes department on level one indicates the pared-down, sober layout adopted by the designers.

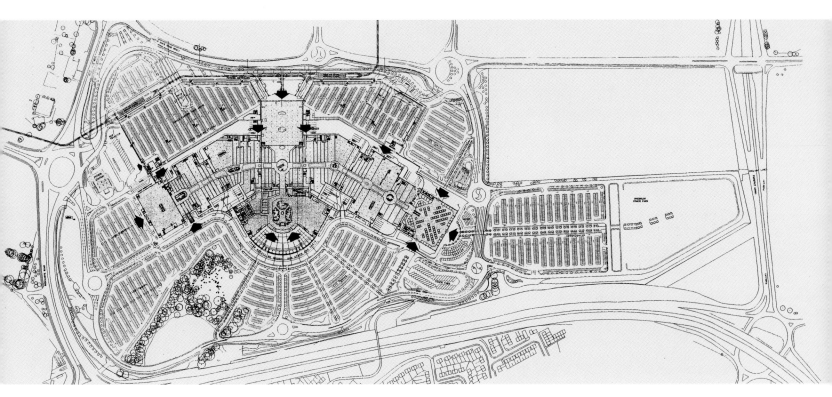

top: Trafford Centre
site plan

above: The approach
to the interior design
was collaborative:
The Conran Design
Partnership created the
chic but informal Spirit
Café using a rich
variety of materials
including glass, natural
screed, light oak and
limestone flooring.
The chairs are classic
Bertoia and the
pendant lights are
by Foscarni.

De Bijenkorf

Amstelveen, The Netherlands, 1998
Architecture:
Atelier Pro / Greig + Stephenson
Interior Design:
Virgile & Stone / Merkx + Girod

De Bijenkorf, founded in 1870, is the most famous department store chain in the Netherlands, with seven branches located in the country's main cities. The Amstelveen branch, which opened in the Rembrandthof shopping centre in 1998, was the company's first new department store for 15 years – and saw De Bijenkorf moving to the city peripheries and experimenting with the role of the anchor store.

For the interior design De Bijenkorf engaged London-based company Virgile & Stone along with Dutch designers Merkx + Girod. De Bijenkorf had already worked successfully with Virgile & Stone on a number of conversion projects in existing department stores. However, for Amstelveen they required something quite different: 'The interior design of the new store moves previous concepts for De Bijenkorf forward into a new era introducing a cleaner, more contemporary backdrop for the merchandise. At 7,500 square metres this is the smallest of De Bijenkorf's stores, so one of the main tasks of the designer was to create a feeling of space using natural light, a neutral palette and an open circulation pattern based around an atrium linking the three floors,' said Virgile & Stone.

In terms of how the department store fitted within the overall ambience of the Rembrandthof, it certainly helped that the

The interior designers were also responsible for the fine main entrance to the centre's anchor store; the La Ruche restaurant sits above the doorway.

British team was also responsible for some of the shopping centre's major architectural features, which they created in collaboration with Dutch architects Atelier Pro – including the main entrances, the public thoroughfares and the interior shop façades. The department store itself has an airy, uncluttered feel. Matt polished steel and glass are the dominant materials, and internal routeways are marked out by discreet zebra stripes on the floor. The De Bijenkorf restaurant La Ruche, located above the external main entrance to the centre, was conceived from the outset as a public attraction in its own right, and so diners do not have to trail through the departments to get to their table.

The Rembrandthof branch was a trial run for the company in a number of respects: as a response to the diversion of customer traffic from the city centres to the commercial peripheries, and as a design formula for future department stores. Working with in-house designers and external architects, Virgile & Stone is currently developing a series of further projects following on from the successful Amstelveen model.

above left: The ground floor accessories department feels light and spacious, with glass, steel and neutrally coloured wood display cases.

above: Virgile and Stone worked with Atelier Pro on the centre's thoroughfares and shop entrances – the steel and glass materials are harmoniously deployed from the foyer through to the department store.

Christian Dior Jean Paul Gaultier Calvin Klein Estée Lauder

opposite: A view over the glass panels of the central atrium shows the clean, open arrangement of the merchandise; circulation routes are indicated by zebra stripes on the floor.

above: The cosmetics department on the ground floor is – like the rest of the store – discreetly ordered and uncluttered.

biographies
credits
index

Biographies

ABD Company
55, 6/1 Sretensky Bulvar,
Moscow 101000, Russia
ABD Company was founded in 1991 by Boris Levyant. Today he works alongside Natalia Sidorova and Lorenz Daniil. Levyant was educated at the Moscow Architectural Institute and worked for both the Department of Development and Urban Environment and 'Dialog' a Soviet-American joint venture before setting-up ABD. Since 1991 projects have included ABC News television studios, Moscow; an exhibition space for Mercedes Benz; a science park for the Moscow State University; various corporate interiors for Western companies in Moscow and a Mega Store. Natalia Sidorova was project architect of the Arsenal store in Moscow. She received a Diploma from the Moscow Architectural Institute and as well as working for ABD is a member of 'Architectural Laboratory', an experimental group which exhibits widely within Russia. Additional projects include an apartment in Moscow (1997); interiors for Comstar Telecommunication Office (1997); a Pizza Hut and KFC outlet in St Petersburg (1997) and the interior of the Fleming UCB Offices in Moscow (1998). Lorenz Daniil is also a member of the Architectural Laboratory and further to his work at ABD has spent periods in the Alsop and Stormer's office in Moscow. He was a project architect on the Arsenal with Sidorova and has also designed interiors for offices and for the Museum of Peace in Moscow.

Harry Allen & Associates
207 Avenue A, New York NY 10009, USA
Harry Allen received a Masters degree in industrial design from the Pratt Institute, New York, then worked for Prescriptives Cosmetics before opening his own studio. He developed a line of furniture, 'Living Systems', which was exhibited at the International Contemporary Furniture Fair and which led to commissions from Sony Plaza NYC and the North Face Store, Chicago. His interior design projects include the Murray Moss shop and More Moss in New York; the Dragonfly Selects jewellery store in Taiwan; the Hushush department store in Tokyo and new offices for both Metropolis magazine and the Guggenheim Museum, New York. Other clients include Donna Karan, Joop Jeans, Dom Perignon and Hennessy Cognac. In addition, Allen has designed a medicine chest for Magis, various articles for Wireworks and lighting for George Kovacs and Ikea. His ceramic foam lamps illustrate his use of new and uncommon materials in the production of an innovative range of products and can be seen in the permanent collection of the Museum of Modern Art, New York.

Ron Arad
62 Chalk Farm Road, London NW1 8AN, UK
Ron Arad was born in Tel Aviv in 1951. He studied at the Jerusalem Academy of Art, and from 1974 to 1979 at the Architectural Association, London. In 1981 he founded One Off with Caroline Thorman. In 1988 he won the Tel Aviv Opera Foyer Interior Competition with C. Norton and S. McAdam. As well as the design and construction of the new One Off design studio in Chalk Farm, London (1991), projects have included furniture design for Poltronova, Vitra, Moroso and Driade; the interiors of restaurants Belgo and Belgo Centraal in London and the winning competition entry for the Adidas Stadium in Paris (unbuilt). In 1994 Arad established the Ron Arad Studio in Como, Italy, to continue the production of limited-edition handmade pieces. He is currently Professor of Furniture Design and Industrial Design at the Royal College of Art in London.

BDG/McColl
24 St John Street, London EC1M 4AY, UK
BDG/McColl (formerly the Business Design Group) was founded in 1962. Specializing in office planning and design, it has offices throughout the UK and also in Frankfurt and Budapest. BDP's clients have included Thomas Cook, American Express, British Gas, Ernst and Young, Smith Kline Beecham, BZW and the UK's Inland Revenue and Departments of Trade and Industry, Environment and Transport. The practice is split into four sectors each cornering different areas of the marketplace. 'BDG McColl Architecture' deals with the design of shopping centres, offices and manufacturing facilities; 'BDG McColl Communications' with graphic design and brand identities as well as staff communications; 'BDG McColl Retail and Leisure' with the development of brand strategy and design of retail and leisure environments; and 'BDG McColl Workplace' offers a service in the space planning, design and construction management of workplace environments. Recent projects include Waterstone's, Oxford Street, London; the South Village at the Bluewater shopping centre in Kent, UK; a shopping centre in Exeter, UK; Barclays Bank in Newark, New Jersey, USA; the Arthur Andersen Business Consulting offices in London, UK and the British Council in Mexico.

BDP – Building Design Partnership
PO Box 4WD, 16 Gresse Street,
London W1A 4WD, UK
BDP was established in 1961 as an interior, graphic and design group specializing in space planning, workplace design and retail design and has been active both in the UK and abroad. Recent/current projects include the interiors of the Adam Opel HQ at Russelsheim near Frankfurt, Germany; the University of Sunderland, UK; fit-outs for British Telecom, the Prudential and Halifax organizations, as well as retail interiors in Germany, Portugal and Spain.

Jacqueline and Henry Boiffils
137 Boulevard Saint Germain,
75006 Paris, France
Husband and wife Jacqueline and Henry Boiffils set up their own architecture and interior design studio in 1984. They specialize in the design of shops, shopping malls, headquarters and salons for the luxury and beauty trade, modernizing the identity of their clients while maintaining the character of their brand names. Customers include the Printemps, chain; Lancôme; Le Club Mediterrannée; Hachette; Christian Lacroix; Rene Derhy and Chanel. They are currently working on a shopping centre in Bangkok for Royal Charoen Krung and jewellery and cosmetic halls at the Galerie Lafayette. In addition, the Boiffils have designed furniture for Editions Quattro, BD Italia and Up & Up, Italy.

Chapman Taylor Partners
364 Kensington High Street,
London W15 8NS, UK
Chapman Taylor Partners (CTP) is an international practice of architects and planners with offices in the UK, Germany, Belgium and Italy. It has been in existence for over 40 years and today is led by 11 partners and undertakes a range of projects from small-scale interiors to public commissions such as airports, hospitals and transport facilities. CTP is also involved in masterplanning, space planning and refurbishment. Major schemes include the Gatwick Airport South Terminal, UK; the Jebel Ali New City, United Arab Emirates; The Lakeside, Thurrock Shopping Mall, UK and the Kuala Lumpur Linear City Development.

David Chipperfield Architects
Cobham Mews, Agar Grove,
London NW1 9SB, UK
David Chipperfield trained at the Architectural Association in London and set up his own practice in 1984. He opened an office in Tokyo three years later where his clients included Issey Miyake and Matsumoto. He now has studios in Berlin and New York and is working on the Neues Museum in Berlin and the Bryant Park Hotel, New York and Shore Club Hotel, Miami. David Chipperfield Architects has undertaken commissions ranging from furniture and interiors to buildings and large-scale urban proposals and has taken part in invited competitions worldwide. It has been selected as the masterplanner of the Museum Island in Berlin and has won the competition to extend the San Michele Cemetery in Venice. Most recently it has been appointed (through competition) as the architect of the new Palace of Justice in Salerno, Italy and the new Museum of Art in Davenport, Iowa, USA. Among other awards, Chipperfield's River and Rowing Museum at Henley-on-Thames, UK, won the 1999 Royal Fine Art Commission Building of the Year Prize and was shortlisted for the 1999 Stirling Prize.

CZWG
17 Bowling Green Lane, London EC1R 0QB, UK
CZWG was founded by Nicholas Campbell, Roger Zogolovitch, Rex Wilkinson and Piers Gough who trained together at the Architectural Association, London, in the late 1960s. The company began by transforming existing buildings but now undertakes new build commissions specializing in innovative private housing. Today it covers a wide spectrum of building types in the public and private sector, projects ranging from urban regeneration and master-

Biographies

planning to exhibition design. Schemes include the National Gallery Extension, London; the National Portrait Gallery, London; the Leonardo Centre, Uppingham, Rutland; Janet Street-Porter's House, Smithfield, London and China Wharf, Bermondsey, London. Piers Gough was appointed CBE for services to architecture in 1998.

Checkland Kindleysides
Charnwood Edge, Cossington,
Leicester LE7 4UZ, UK
Established in 1979, Checkland Kindleysides specializes in strategic design for global brands. Its approach combines many aspects of design work, graphics, visual merchandising and interior disciplines, to create powerful and compelling merchandising and identities. Clients include Levi Strauss, Manchester United FC, Ray-Ban, Rolls-Royce & Bentley Motor Cars and Porsche Design

Conran & Partners (was CD Partnership)
22 Shad Thames, London SE1 2YU, UK
The architecture, interior and graphic design practice was founded by Terence Conran and employs over 20 designers and architects. Projects undertaken include the design of the Longman Publishing Group's headquarters in Harlow, Essex, UK; the London Conran restaurants Mezzo and Quaglino's; the cafe and lido on two levels of Celbrity Cruises' super liner launched in 1995; The Trieste Hotel in Vienna and Selfidges' restaurants in London and Manchester. Graphic projects include the full design and implementation of the corporate identity for Cabouchon, the UK's leading fashion jeweller, and a development programme for Providence Capitol's product literature.

Design Associates
Winterstrasse 4, 81543 Munich, Germany
Design Associates was founded by Uwe Binnberg and Stephan Lang in 1993. Binnberg worked for Frederic Fischer in Los Angeles and Warner Brothers Filmpark where he was involved in the design of science fiction scenarios. Lang collaborated with Skidmore Owings and Merrill, Stiedle and Partners and Architekturbüro Strehle in Munich. From 1992 to 1995 he was assistant to Professor Hughes in Munich. Design Associates specializes in product design and furniture prototypes as well as the design of office spaces, shops, sound studios and small-scale architectural projects. The pair have recently worked on a building for the insurance company Arag in Munich.

Douglas Design Associates Incorporated
35 N. Arroyo Parkway No. 200, Pasadena,
California, CA 91103, USA
Douglas Design specializes in bringing fantasy to hotel, casino and resort design, from recalling the lost grandeur of the Louisanna steamboat at the Hyatt's Elgin Riverboat resort, New Orleans to recreating an old Roman marketplace at the Forum Shops at Caesar's Palace, Las Vegas. The company has eighteen years experience in the leisure industry and in combining interior design with spectacle. Other projects include the complete restoration of the Stardust Hotel and Casino, the Buffet at the Fremont Hotel, the Tony Romas Restaurant and the Tres Lobos Restaurant in addition to work for ITT Sheraton and Hilton Hotels Corporation.

ECE Projektmanagement
Heegbarg 30, 22391 Hamburg, Germany
The ECE Group manages large scale business properties, with companies in Germany, Poland, Hungary and the Czech Republic. Specializing in planning, implementation, development, leasing and management, ECE has designed offices, retail premises and special purpose real-estate and is responsible for managing 60 shopping centres in Germany. Over 1,300 specialists are employed to assess new locations, develop utilization concepts and work on the realization of building projects.

Massimiliano Fuksas Architect
30 Piazza del Monte di Pieta 00186, Italy
The architect and town planner Massimiliano Fuksas was born in Rome in 1944. He holds a degree in Architecture from 'La Sapienza' University in Rome where he later taught and carried out research in the History of Architecture Department. Since his award-winning design for the reception point at the Musee des Graffitis, the landscape arrangement of the entrance of the Grotto of Niaux (1993) and the Europark Mall, Salzburg, three years later, he has been building up an international reputation for his innovative and startling designs. The Ministry of Culture and Communication in France conferred him the honour of 'Officer de l'Ordre des Arts et des Lettres de la Republique Francaise in 1988. He is the director of the Architecture section of the Venice Biennale until 2001 and in June 1999 won the Grand Prix d'Architecture in Paris. Recent schemes and projects on site include the 'Twin Towers' offices for Wienerberger Vienna (2001), a new archeological museum built into the former Aldobrandini stable, Rome (1999), the Peace Centre in Jaffa (commissioned 1998); the pedestrian bridge and travel park in Vlotho-Exter, Germany (in design); the tourist port 'Marina di Stabis', Naples, Italy (in design) and the new market hall in the Piazza della Repubblica.

Rupert Gardner Design AB
Banérgatan 10, S–115 23 Stockholm, Sweden
Founded in 1985, Rupert Gardner Design AB is a design office with an international practice based in Stockholm, Sweden. It works on a wide range of projects from offices, shops and private homes to restaurants, cruise ships and retail chain stores. Major projects in recent years include clothing shops in Sweden, Norway and Germany; the Stockman Department Store in Finland; 35 Tella telephone shops and offices throughout Sweden and 70 Carolls hamburger restaurants in Finland. Rupert Gardner was born in the UK and studied at the Royal College of Art, London, under Norman Foster and James Stirling. He worked for Ricardo Bofill's office in Barcelona before moving to Sweden in 1976.

GCA Arquitectos Associats
Cl Valencia 289, 08009 Barcelona, Spain
Founded in 1986 by Josep Juanpere and Antoni Pulg and later joined by Josep Riu, Jesús Hernando and Arturo de la Maza, GCA now employs a team of 50 professionals including architects and interior designers. Having started out as an interior design office, GCA has developed a comprehensive approach to architecture integrating interior design and furnishing in every project. It has worked extensively on existing and listed buildings using design strategies which respect the characters of existing buildings. GCA also works on the creation of corporate images through design for companies as varied as Citybank, Next Generation and Yanko, as well as projects for schools, cinemas and hotels.

Studio Iosa Ghini
Via Caprarie 7, 40124 Bologna, Italy
Massimo Iosa Ghini was born in Borgo Tossignano, Italy in 1959 and graduated in architecture from Milan Polytechnic. Before working with Ettore Sottsass and Memphis in 1986, he was involved in drawing cartoons for international magazines. In 1987 he launched his first collection, Dynamic, for Moroso which received awards worldwide. Interior design projects include the planning of the fashion chain Fiorucci and the planning and design of the Renault Italy showrooms, shops for Swatch and the flagship store and subsequent outlets for Superga. Since 1992 he has held two major retrospectives, one at the Steininger Gallery, Munich and the second at the Inspiration Gallery in the Axis Building, Tokyo. Iosa Ghini is also involved in the design of eye-wear, consumer electronics, lighting, bathroom and kitchen suites, and is responsible for the exhibition stands and selected showrooms for Ferrarri and Maserati. In 1995 he was invited to an international congress of architects organized by IFI at Nagoya, Japan (the only Italian ever to be given this honour). He is a member of the ABN (Global Business Network).

Henn Architekten Ingenieure
Augustenstrasse 54, D-80333 Munich, Germany
Henn Architekten Ingenieure is a large international practice based in Germany. It has enjoyed a long-standing relationship with the Volkswagen company and has recently completed the vast Autostadt project.

John Herbert Partnership (JHP)
8 Berkley Road, Primose Hill,
London NW1 8YR, UK
Founded in 1979, JHP specializes in the creation of corporate identities, combining interior architecture and its work in graphic communication with design innovation and commercial awareness. JHP has worked with Eurotunnel; Zurich Airport; the Royal National Lifeboat Institution; British Gas; the Tower of London; Boots the Chemist; Heineken; Dolcis;

Biographies

Selfridges; Calvin Klein and Ralph Lauren. Awards include the Design Effectiveness Award of 1989 for the Coventry Building Society; Store of the Year Award in 1996 for Selfridges Trafford Centre, Manchester, UK, and the Civic Trust award in 1995 for the Fountains Abbey Visitor Centre, Yorkshire, UK.

Herman Hertzberger
Postbus 74665, 1070 BR Amsterdam,
The Netherlands
Herman Hertzberger was born in Amsterdam in 1932. He studied at the Technical University of Delft and graduated in 1958, founding his own practice the same year. He has taught at the Academy of Architecture in Amsterdam and was Professor at the Technical University of Delft as well as Visiting Professor at several American and Canadian universities and the University of Geneva. Today he teaches at the Berlage Institute in Amsterdam. He is an honorary member of Art and Architecture academies in England, Scotland, Germany, France and Italy, and in 1999 was awarded the 'Ridder in de Orde van de Nederlandse Leeuw' – the Dutch Knighthood. Since 1958 his practice has completed numerous private and institutional residential schemes, a series of primary schools and offices, and from the early 1990s has undertaken progressively larger projects which include the Centre for Art and Music and the 'De Nieuwe Veste' Library in Breda, the extension of the Vanderveen Department Store and the Montessori College Oost. He is currently working on various architectural projects and urban design concepts such as the design peninsula in Tel Aviv; masterplans for areas of Berlin, Munich and Almere, and a theatre in Helsingor, Denmark.

Hosker Moore & Kent
20 Golden Square, London W1R 4AU, UK
Hosker Moore & Kent was founded in 1990 and specializes in interior design, architecture, brand focusing and creating design solutions. The partners include designers Louise Hosker, a graduate of Manchester University with 14 years design experience and a member on the judging panel of the 1995 Design Awards, and Peter Kent who graduated from Kingston College of Art and has previously worked as an industrial designer for Terence Conran. Peter Moore, the practice's architect, graduated from Canterbury College of Art and Design with a first class diploma in Architecture. His previous projects with David Davies & Associates include the RIBA award winning Next Headquarters in Leicester, UK. Kishore Patel, the fourth founder member of the practice, comes from the business sector and works on the strategic management of the partnership. Hosker Moore & Kent has specialized in the fashion retail and luxury brand arena, with commissions from Valentino, Moschino, Furia, Etam, Boots the Chemist, the Hyde Park Hotel,London, and the new Harvey Nichols store in Leeds, UK. The practice is also active in the office sector, having completed works for The Mill Facility, London, Redwood Publishing and Clerical and Medical.

Daryl Jackson Interiors
35 Little Bourke Street, Melbourne,
Victoria 3000, Australia
Daryl Jackson has offices in Melbourne, Sydney, Canberra and Brisbane and international branches in London and Berlin. In London, the practice has recently built a series of insertions into the existing railway arches underneath Cannon Street Station creating the 'Cannons Health Club'. Other leisure projects include the Welsh Garden Festival Pavilion and the Cedars Health and Leisure Club in Richmond which received the RIBA regional award. It has also completed various housing projects along the River Thames for the London Docklands Authority ranging from an adaptive re-use of redundant warehousing to a new wall of housing near Tower Bridge. Daryl Jackson has undertaken a heritage redevelopment office project in Budapest, Hungary, housing and offices in Potsdam, Germany, and has won a housing/urban planning competition in Brandenberg, Germany. The office in Berlin is currently documenting a major residence in Berlin and exploring a redevelopment housing study for the site of the 1936 Olympic Games Village.

Ben Kelly Design
10 Stoney Street, London SE1 9AD, UK
Ben Kelly Design was established in London in 1977 by designer Ben Kelly, who graduated from the Royal College of Art, London, in 1974, having studied environmental/interior design. Kelly's early projects include work for Malcolm McLaren/The Sex Pistols and Lynne Frank: major designs number the Hacienda nightclub and venue, Manchester; the Dry 201 bar and restaurant, Manchester; the 4AD record company headquarters, London; offices for Rainey Kelly Campbell Roafe advertising agency in London and new offices for Lynne Frank. BKD has also worked on the exhibition design for the 1996 BBC Design Awards and the Glasgow International Festival of Design 1996 Exhibition. It has recently completed the Basement at the Science Museum, London; the British Design Council Offices in London and a flagship store scheme for a major clothing company. Kelly has taught interior/3D design at Kingston University, UK, and acts as external assessor at the Glasgow School of Art. Plans and Elevations, a book on the practice, was published in 1990. Patrick McKinney and Richard Blurton, project architects on the Halford stores joined BDK in 1996 and 1997 and studied at Middlesex University and Kingston University respectively. They have worked on numerous schemes including the Design Council offices, True Stories (a touring exhibition in Japan) and 100% Design at Earls Court 2, London, UK.

Kister Scheithauer Gross
Schaafenstrasse 25, 50676 Cologne, Germany
Kister Scheithauer Gross was founded in 1988 and now has offices in both Cologne and Dessau, Germany. Although it does undertake some smaller residential schemes, its main area of expertise lies in larger scale buildings including homes for the elderly, industrial outlets, universities, institutes, museums and libraries. It also works on concepts for urban development, masterplans and housing developments. Its steel Hall for the Hulden firm in Duren and the Mediapark in Cologne both won the 2000 Award for Exemplary Buildings in Nordrhein-Westfalen 2000.

Kohn Pedersen Fox Associates
111 W 57th Street, New York, NY 10019, USA
Kohn Pedersen Fox Associates was founded in 1976 by Eugene Kohn, Williams Pedersen and Sheldon Fox. It now employs over 325 people and has opened offices in London (1989) and Tokyo (1995). The firm offers a full architecture and master-planning programme for clients in both the public and private sectors and its portfolio includes mixed-use, corporate and institutional master plans; investment office buildings, retail development, entertainment complexes, and corporate headquarters; educational, institutional and health care facilities; hotels, resorts and conference centres; residences; transportation facilities and museums. KPF has been the recipient of many major national and international awards and in 1990 became the youngest firm to be honoured with the highest accolade of the American Institute of Architects, the AIA Architectural Firm Award.

Krueck & Sexton Architects
221 West Erie, Chicago, Illinois 60610, USA
Founded in 1979 by Ron Krueck and Mark Sexton, both from the Illinois Institute of Technology, this Chicago-based practice provides a full service from architecture and planning to interior design and is recognized for design innovation, knowledge of the building arts and a rigorous approach to management and construction. Krueck and Sexton has acquired a reputation for design solutions which combine functionality with the flexibility to accommodate growth and change, and has won awards from various engineering and technical societies. The practice has completed projects ranging from the Christies and Thonet Showrooms and the Joseph Cornell Gallery to the World Savings Bank, as well as offices and residential work.

Eric Kuhne & Associates
York House, 23 Kingsway,
London WC2B 6UJ, UK
Eric Kuhne and Associates is an international design consultancy which combines architecture with landscape and civic arts. Eric R. Kuhne is an architect, industrial designer, graphic designer, essayist and lecturer. He holds a BA in art and architecture from Rice University, Texas, and a Masters of Architecture from Princeton University, New Jersey. Recent projects include a riverfront development in Fort Wayne, Indiana, a residence on Chesapeake Bay, an office and entertainment complex in Sydney, Australia and the Bluewater shopping complex in Kent, UK.

Mahmoudieh Design
Kurfurstendamm 37, 10719 Berlin, Germany
Yasmine Mahmoudieh was born in Germany. She studied Art History in Florence, Architecture at the

Biographies

Ecole D'Ingenieur in Geneva, Interior Design at the College of Notre Dame in Belmont as well as Architecture and Interior Design at the University of California in Los Angeles where she received her Diploma. She worked for various architectural practices in the USA before co-founding The Architectural Design Group International in 1986 and her own company in Los Angeles. Today, Mahmoudieh Design has offices in Hamburg and Berlin and is due to open a branch in London. Mahmoudieh Design works on restaurants, exhibition and fair stands, exclusive boarding houses and furniture, as well as undertaking the interior design of hotels and office buildings. Recent projects include the Kempinski Hotel, Bad Saarow, Germany; the Millennium Center in Budapest, Hungary; offices for Garbe KG in Hamburg, Germany; 'The Factory' in Berlin (conversion of an old mill into galleries, restaurants, offices and lofts); the Gordon Eckhard Production Studios in Hollywood and the renovation of a former Beatles' house, the De La Bruyere-Residence in Beverly Hills, Los Angeles. Current projects include renovation of the SAS Royal Hotel in Copenhagen; the interior design of a new hotel for disabled people on the outskirts of Berlin; the office concept and corporate design for a renowned American insurance company in Germany and a shopping centre outside London.

Maurice Mentjens
Martinusstraat 20, 6123 BS Holtum,
The Netherlands
Maurice Mentjens studied the design of metals and synthetic materials at the Academy for Visual Arts in Maastricht, The Netherlands, and was awarded his degree in 1988. He then went on to receive a further degree in Architectural Design, and spent a summer session at the Domus Academy in Milan in 1990. He has completed various retail interiors within The Netherlands, most notably the chain of outlets for Sirius. He has also designed the Taste and Scent Laboratory in the Bonnefantenmuseum in Maastricht, as well as watches for Milus and Ventura, lamps for Luxo, desk accessories for Aston Martin and tables for Gallina Design. He is a guest lecturer at the Academy for Visual Arts in Maastricht and for the Open University in Heerlen.

Meyer en van Schooten Architecten
Stadhouderskade 115, 1073 AX Amsterdam,
The Netherlands
Meyer en van Schooten Architecten was founded by Roberto Meyer and Jeroen W. van Schooten in 1984. They both studied at the Technical College of Architecture, Amsterdam, followed by the Academies of Architecture in Amsterdam and Arnhem, graduating in 1990 and 1991 respectively. They specialize in housing schemes and urban planning and have also completed various offices and retail outlets in The Netherlands. Both partners lecture nationally, and the practice's work has been exhibited widely within The Netherlands, most recently at the Architecture Centre in Amsterdam.

In 1999 they took part in the International Property Market Fair in Cannes, France.

Murphy/Jahn Inc.
35 East Wacker Drive, Chicago,
Illinois 60601, USA
Murphy/Jahn Inc. was established over 50 years ago and is still headed by Helmut Jahn who is responsible for the design of every project undertaken by the firm which now employs over 80 people, six of whom are principal architects. The practice maintains a diverse client profile from private individual to corporate, institutional and governmental bodies although it is best known for its large, high-rise and commercial structures which have been publicized in leading national and international periodicals.

Torsten Neeland Industrial Design
61 Redchurch Street, London E2 7DJ, UK
Torsten Neeland graduated from the Industrial Design University of Fine Arts in Hamburg, Germany. He specializes in furniture and lighting design with clients such as Anita, Ansorg, Anthologie Quartett, Rosenthal and Authentics. His interior architecture projects reflect his belief in the reduction of formal design to the minimum and the importance of subtle lighting effects. He has shown his work in joint shows throughout Europe and has held one-man exhibitions in Hamburg and Dusseldorf.

Pei Cobb Freed & Partners
600 Madison Avenue, New York, NY 10022, USA
Ieoh Ming Pei was born in China in 1917. He moved to the USA to study architecture at the Massachusetts Institute of Technology and received a Bachelor of Architecture degree in 1940. He then studied at the Harvard Graduate School of Design under Walter Gropius – at the same time teaching in the faculty as assistant professor – and gained a Masters degree in 1946. In 1955, Pei formed I. M. Pei and Associates, which became I. M. Pei and Partners in 1989. The practice has designed over 150 projects in the USA and abroad, more than half of which have won awards and citations. As well as working for corporate and private investment clients, the practice has executed numerous commissions for public authorities and religious, educational and cultural institutions. Its most important buildings include the Bank of China, Hong Kong; The East West Wing of the National Gallery of Washington, DC; the Grand Louvre in Paris and the United States Holocaust Memorial Museum, Washington, DC. Works recently completed or on site include the Rock and Roll Hall of Fame and Museum, Cleveland, Ohio; Trinity College in Dublin; the World Trade Center Hotel in Barcelona; the Jerusalem Museum in Israel and the United states Air Force Memorial in Arlington National Cemetery. Following the retirement of I.M. Pei in 1990, leadership of the firm has continued under Henry Cobb and James Ingo Freed in collaboration with Michael Flynn and George Miller. The company expanded in 1999 to include two additional partners, Ian Bader and Yvonne Szeto.

Pentagram Design/Architecture
204 Fifth Avenue, New York, NY 10010, USA
Pentagram Design was founded in 1972 in London and has since expanded to include offices in New York (1978), San Francisco (1986), Hong Kong (1994) and Austin, Texas (1995). Pentagram Architecture (US) was founded by James Biber in 1991 and specializes in residential interiors, restaurants, retail outlets, offices, health clubs and exhibition design. James Biber AIA graduated from Cornell University's College of Architecture, Art and Planning and worked for various American architectural practices before founding his own company in 1984. He has taught classes in Architecture at Cornell and Syracuse Universities, as well as at the Parson's School of Design, New York. His designs have been recognized with major awards, from among others, the New York State Association of Architects and the New York Chapter of the American Institute of Architects. Projects for Pentagram Architecture include Sullivan's Restaurant and Broadcast Lounge, New York, the Good Diner and Bolo. Clients include Disney Imagineering, Plus One Fitness and the Cooper-Hewitt National Design Museum. Daniel Weil became a partner of Pentagram in 1992. He studied at the University of Buenos Aires, Argentina, and received an MA in Industrial Design at London's Royal College of Art, where he later became Professor of Industrial and Vehicle Design.

Sauerbruch Hutton Architects
Lehrter Strasse 57, 10557 Berlin, Germany
Sauerbruch Hutton Architects was founded in 1989 by Louisa Hutton and Matthias Sauerbruch. Hutton holds a BA (Hons) from Bristol University and a Diploma from the Architectural Association, London, while Sauerbruch was educated at the HDK Berlin before studying at the Architectural Association, London, where he was Unit Master from 1985–90. Since 1995 he has been a Professor at the Technical University in Berlin. Today, the practice has offices in London and Berlin and built works range from office and commercial buildings, laboratories and production halls, to housing, restoration and conservation projects as well as projects in the field of urban design. Notable schemes include the low energy high rise office block, GSW-Headquarters, Berlin; laboratories, offices and a production hall for Photonics, Berlin; offices for the Ministry of the Environment, Dessau; a police and fire station, Berlin; the 'L', 'H', and 'N' houses in London and the Zumtobel Staff Lichtzentrum in Berlin.

Claudio Silvestrin Architects
392 St John Street, London WEC1, UK
Claudio Silvestrin was born in 1954 and trained in Milan at AG Fronzoni. He completed his studies at the Architectural Association in London where he now lives and works. He teaches at the University of London's Bartlett School of Architecture and at the Ecole Superieure d'Art Visuels in Lausanne, Switzerland. He has realized projects worldwide and some of his most important works include shops for

Giorgio Armani (Paris), the offices, shops and home for Calvin Klein (Paris, Milan and New York) and works for museums and art galleries.

Springmann Architektur GmbH
Urbanstrasse 31, 73207 Plochingen, Germany
Heinz Springmann has worked as a freelance architect since 1979 and now employs 27 members of staff on a variety of projects including industrial and commercial premises, offices and residential projects and refurbishments. Springmann has designed premises for companies as diverse as Volksbank, Sarnatech-Schenk, Burger King and Daimler Benz, as well as public buildings including the Martin-Luther School in Wittenberg, Germany, and a Catholic community centre in Plochingen, Germany. He is most widely recognized for the realization of many special building projects by the artist Friedensreich Hundertwasser.

Takenaka Corporation
1–13, 4-chome, Hommachi, Chuo-ku, Osaka, 541-0053, Japan
Takenaka is a large corporate architectural, planning and engineering firm with offices in Japan, USA, Poland, UK and France. Having celebrated its 100th anniversary in 1999, the company has taken a front seat in researching and implementing solutions to global environmental and construction safety issues within a 300-strong research and development team. Recent projects include Procter & Gamble's Japan Headquarters of 1993; the Fukuoka and Nagoya Domes; the Tokyo Opera City and the New National Theatre in Tokyo. Takenaka has received numerous awards for design, construction, innovation and safety including the first Architectural Institute of Japan Award for the adoption of Total Quality Control in the construction industry, and the Minister of Construction Prize of Energy-Saving Building in both 1990 and 1991 with the IBM Japan Yamato Research Institute and Mitsui Warehouse Hakozaki Building.

Umdasch Shop-Concept
Amstetten, Austria
Established over 100 years ago, Umdasch Shop-Concept is one of Europe's largest shopfitting and design companies. It supplies standard elements to and creates concepts for a leading international clientele which includes World of Sport, Harrods, Argos, C&A, Lust for Life and Woolworths. It specializes in all areas of retail marketing from department stores to factory outlet and from boutique to hyper-market, as well as offering a consultancy service on retail marketing, operations, shop design and presentation.

O. M. Ungers & Partners
Marienstrasse 10, 10117 Berlin, Germany
The internationally acclaimed architecture office of Professor O. M. Ungers consists of two Germany-based offices: one in Cologne and the other in Berlin. The Cologne office is staffed by 15 licensed architects, and its major focus lies in design development and working drawings. The Berlin office has the same structure with about 10 employees, specializing in the development of trade fair complexes with exhibition spaces, restaurants, hotels, offices, retail spaces and congress centres. There is, in addition, a cooperation office in New York, USA. Besides design and construction planning, the practice also addresses urbanistic issues. A small group of people works on object design, which allows for work across the spectrum, from an urbanistic proposal to interior design.

Jeff Vandeberg
873 Broadway, Suite 601, New York, NY 10003, USA
Jeff Vandeberg has been in practice in New York since 1973. He received a B.Arch from the University of Nebraska and undertook graduate studies in architecture at the University of Michigan, Ann Arbor, before moving to New York to work with Marcel Breuer and Associates. He has taught architectural design at the Pratt Institute, New York, and his work has been widely exhibited and published. In 1996, 1998 and 1999 he was the recipient of the S.A.R.A. Award for Design Excellence. Vandeberg Architects specializes in large-scale conversions, unique manufacturing processes, e-commerce, commercial and residential projects.

Virgile & Stone Associates
25 Store Street, South Crescent, London WC1E 7BL, UK
Virgile & Stone is an international design consultancy specializing in retail, restaurant, hotel, showroom, leisure and workplace environments. The firm was founded in 1980 by Carlos Virgile and Nigel Stone since which time it has built up a client base which includes Hugo Boss, Wedgwood, Groupe Chez Gerard and De Bijenkorf chain of stores in The Netherlands. Recent schemes include new department stores in Germany for Breuninger and for De Bijenkorf in Amstelveen; a new concept for Chez Gerard restaurants; retail projects for Heal's, London; a restaurant and bar for restaurateur Stephen Bull and an exhibition showcase for Patek Philippe, the world renowned watchmaker, for the Basel Fair in Switzerland. It is currently undertaking the design of the main restaurant of the Oberoi Towers Hotel in Mumbai, India as well as an extensive graphics project for a themed restaurant within the same hotel. Other schemes have emerged since its involvement on the innovative retail concept for Schipol Airport's Central Lounge which opened in September 1999. Together with Benthem Crouwel (the airport's Dutch architects), Virgile and Stone is now involved in the development of a new shopping centre in Amsterdam, The Villa Arena. In addition, it has been commissioned by Anderson Consulting to work on the interiors of their new headquarters alongside Sir Norman Foster and space planners Studios.

Wood and Zapata Inc.
100 South Street, Boston, MA 02111, USA
Wood & Zapata was created by Ben Wood and Carlos Zapata. The practice offers a master planning, urban design, architectural and interior design service throughout the United States and internationally. Current projects comprise the international concourse at Miami International Airport; the rehabilitation and new construction of two city blocks in Shanghai; the Sundance Cinema in Philadelphia and a series of projects for the Chicago Bears, including their new open-air stadium. Wood and Zapata has received several design awards and its work has been published extensively throughout the world.

Hideo Yasui Atelier
Nansai Haitu 604, 6-1-32 Minami-Aoyama, Minato-ku, Tokyo, Japan
Hideo Yasui received his architecture degree from Aichi Institute of Technology, Japan, in 1981. Before founding his own design firm in Tokyo in 1986, he worked at Takimitsu Azurra Architects and Associates and the Setsuo Kitaoka Design Studio. Among his awards are the Silver (1988) and Gold (1989) Prizes of the NASOP Lighting Contest; Special Prize (1992) and Award of Excellence (1997) from the Inter Intra Space Design Selection; and a 1996 Performance Award of the JCD Awards.

Robert Young Associates
2608 Inwood Road, Dallas, Texas 75235, USA
Robert Young Associates was founded nearly 40 years ago as a store design consultancy. It offers expert advise as well as undertaking its own store planning, interior, fixture and lighting design. Its clients include Bloomingdales, Neiman Marcus, Bon Marche, Tiffany & Co and Fossil, for whom they create flag ship stores and renovations.

Credits

Advanced Cique
Tokyo, Japan
Interior Designer: Yasui Hideo
Client: Olizonty Co. Ltd. Main Contractor: Isimaru Co. Ltd. Glazing: Mihoya Glass Co. Ltd. Furniture Design: Makoto Araki.

Giorgio Armani
Paris, France
Interior Designer: Claudio Silvestrin Architects
Client: Giorgio Armani. Project Team: Claudio Silvestrin, Simona Pieri, Douglas Tuck. General Contractor: Alpha International. Furniture Contractor: Contract. Furniture and Lighting Design: Claudio Silvestrin.

Arsenal
Moscow, Russia.
Interior Designer: ABD Company
Client: VVV. Project Team: Natalia Sidorova, Lorenz Daniil, Boris Levyant. Main Contractor: Bioinjector (store equipment). Lights: Targetti.

Autostadt
Wolfsburg, Germany
Architect: Henn Architekten Ingenieure
Client: Volkswagen AG; Autostadt Wolfsburg. Project Managers: Drees & Sommer. Participating Planners: Alfredo Arribas (Seat); Arthesia; Jack Rousse Associates (Konzernforum, ZeitHaus); Furneaux Stewart (Bentley, VW Pavilion); Confino (Audi); Bellprat Associates, (Lamborghini); Grüntuch/Ernst(VW Pavilion); KSS Architects (Bentley); Sipek (Skoda). Interior Design: Andrée Putman (Ritz-Carlton Hotel); Tony Chi & Associates (Restaurant KonzernForum); Jordan Mozer Associates (Restaurant and Retail ZeitHaus); United Designers (Restaurant, KonzernForum); Virgile & Stone Associates (Restaurant KundenCenter, Retail Konzernforum). Landscaping: WES & Partner. Technical Fit-out: Heinz, Stockfisch, Grabis & Partner (KundenCenter, Fahrzeeutürme, Bentley, Skoda, Outlet); HL-Technik AG (KonzernForum, VW Pavilion, VW-Nutzfahrzeuge); Müller und Bleher (Zeithaus, VW-Nutzfahrzeuge); Jaeger, Mornhinweg + Partner (Zeithaus, HLS, VW-Nutzfahrzeuge, HLS); Kuehn, Bauer Partner (Ritz-Carlton Hotel, Audi, Seat, VW Pavilion). Façade: Hussak; Schalm. Construction: Bendorf + Partner (Ritz-Carlton Hotel, Zeithaus, VW Pavilion, VW-Nutzfahrzeuge); Dröge, Baade + Partner (Konzernforum); Scholz & Partner (Audi, Seat); Windels, Timm, Morgen (KundenCenter, Dachtragwerk, Pylon); Leonhardt, Andrä und Partner (Brücke Mittellandkanal). Infrastructure: IGH. Acoustics: Müller BBM. Kitchen Design: CFP Gastro AG; LZ-Plan.

Bloomingdales Aventura
Miami, Florida, USA
Architect: Kohn Pedersen Fox Associates
Interior Designer: Robert Young Associates
Client: Federated Department Stores Inc. Project Team: Kevin Kennon (Design Principal), Marianne Kwik, Nicola Wallter (Design Team Leaders), Nathan Clark Corser, Andreas Hausler, David Weinberg (Project Managers), Angeline Ho, David Kaplan (Co-ordination Leaders), Elina Cardet, Luke Fox, Tomas Hernandez, Michael Marcolini, Widia Ranti, Lisa Ross, Aida Saleh. General Contractor: Whiting-Turner. Consultants: Heitman & Associates (exterior wall). Engineers: Shenberger & Associates (structural); Cosentini Associates (mechanical, electrical); LAW Engineering (civil).

Bluewater
Dartford, Kent, UK
Architect: Eric Kuhne & Associates
Client: Lend Lease. Project Architect: Benoy Architects. Associate Architects: Brettell Jackson & Associates (HoF); Brooker Flynn Architects (JLP); GHM Rock Townsend (Multiplex); Leach Rhodes Walker (C&A); RRTKL (M&S); Design Solution (mall finishes concept); Fitch (Waterstones); BDG McColl (South Village). Main Contractor: Bluewater Construction Management. Environmental Consultant: Battle McCarthy. Quantity Surveyor: Cyril Sweett & Partners. Consulting Engineers: Halcrow. Acoustics: Sandy Brown Associates. Lighting: Speirs & Major. Landscape: Townshend. Civil/Structural Engineer: Waterman Partnership. Roof/glazing: EAG; Prater Roofing. Roof membrane: Sarnafil. Aluminium roof: Hoogovens. Atrium Glazing: Sky Systems/Space Decks. Glazing/curtain wall: Dane Architectural; Stewart Frazier. Doors/ironmongery: Hillson. Limestone floors: Steinindustrie Vetter. Balustrading: Alan Dawson Associates; Barker Shepley; Tecscreen. Ceilings: Riverside Mouldings; Clarke & Fenn; Jonathan James; Thermofelt. Metalwork: Gravesham Engineering. Faux stone painting: Lucas. Column finishes: Armourcoat. Signage: Drakard & Humble. Decorative Panels: Original Prop Shop. Glass Bridges: T&W Ide. Fabric Panels: Architen. Joinery: Abacus; Henry Venables. Metalwork: Littlehampton Welding; AR Dibley. Lighting: Zumtobel Staff; Enliten; We-Es; Oldham; Philips; Wila.

Chelsea Market
New York, New York, USA
Architect: Vandeberg Architects
Client: ATC Management. Project Team: Jeff Vandeberg (Principal), Jason Popkin, Jon Wallter, Misa Radulof. Structural Engineers: Goldstein Consulting Engineers. Mechanical Engineers: Copeland Engineers. Sculptor: Mark Mennin.

De Barones
Breda, The Netherlands
Architects: CZWG Architects / Kraaijvanger Urbis
Client: MAB Groep bv; Vroom and Dreesmann; Municipality of Breda. Project Team: Rex Wilkinson; Ray Stuart. Site Architect: Kraaijvanger Urbis. Main Contractor: Heijmans Bouw. Structural Engineer: Grabowsky & Poort BV. Services Engineer: Smits Van Burgst. Graphic Design: Cuba Design. Construction Manager: Kats & Waalwijk. Terracotta: Ibstock Hathernware. Lighting Consultant: Lighting Design Partnership. Rooflights: Kalwall. Custom Made Door Furniture: Re:Form. Terracotta: Ibstock Hathernware. Bronze Door Handles: Re:Form. Rooflights: Kalwell.

De Bijenkorf
Amstelveen, The Netherlands
Architects: Atelier Pro / Grieg + Stephenson
Interior Designers: Virgile & Stone Associates / Merkx & Girod BV Architekten
Client: De Bijenkorf. Store Design: Virgile & Stone Associates. Collaborating Architects: Merkx & Girod BV Architekten (lower ground floor, homewares department and first floor La Ruche restaurant); Greig & Stephenson (architectural shell, vertical circulation and access points). Main Contractor: Benschop BV.

Dick
Esslingen, Germany
Architect: Heinz M. Springmann
Client: Weststadt. Project Team: Daniel Göhner, Oliver Graf, Thomas Groll, Armin Kilx, Robert Lubik, Martin Moosmann, Bernhard Nagl, Alberto Policano, Andrea Schmid, Karl-Heinz Schmidt, Gaston Stoff, Beate Storr. Cinema Architect: Rainer J. Gottschling, dpo Büro. Quantity Surveyor/Project Control: Matthias Göller, Ingenieurbüro. Geologist: Dr Markus J. Biehler. Stress Analyst: Fritz Deufel, Ingenieurgesellschaft Deufel mbH. Statics Control: Dr. Ing. H. Meissnest, Ing.-Büro für Bauwesen.Services Engineer: IPS Ingenieurpartnerschaft.

Emporium
Bangkok, Thailand
Architect/Interior Designers: Jacqueline & Henry Boiffils
Client: The Mall Group Co. Suppliers: Thaikoei International, Rider Hunt, Landmark Entertainment Group, Palmer & Turner Ltd., RTKL International Ltd., Thai Hazama Corporation Ltd., PU Associates Co. Ltd., PD International, WRT Corporation, CEDA Co. Ltd., EMC Engineering Ltd., STS Engineering Ltd.

Europark
Salzburg, Austria
Architect: Massimiliano Fuksas
Client: SPAR Warenhandels AG. Project Team: Massimiliano Fuksas, Concetta Schepis, Dietmar Haupt, Ralph Bock, Suzanne Gruner. General Contractor: Takenaka Europe GmbH. Structural Engineer: Vasko & Partner. Glass façade: Focchi srl. Lighting Consultant: Bartenbbach.

The Forum Shops
Las Vegas, Nevada, USA
Architect: Marnell Corrao Associates
Interior Designer: Dougall Design Associates
Client: The Gordon Co.; Melvin Simon & Associates. General Contractor and Implementation Architect: Marnell Corrao Associates. Project Management: Melvin Simon & Associates. Streetscape flooring: Arcon. Fountain of the Gods Statuary; Goddess of Foruna: Art Sculpture and Production. Marble

Credits

Flooring: Catello Tile & Marble Contractors. Fixtures, house: Cederquist. Animatronic character movement, Festival Fountain: Creative Presentations Inc. Store façade statuary: Design Toscano. Artwork and Trompe L'Oeil: Douglas Bouman and Associates; Elizabeth Sadoff and Associates; Magia Inc. Terry Peterson. Metal details: Eurocraft. Reinforced gyp fibre and concrete: G&G Manufacturing. Mosaic tiles: Hastings. Lighting design: Imero Fiorentino Associates. Waterworks, Fountain of the Gods, Festival Fountain: Laser Media Inc. Lighting fixtures: Premiere chandelier. Rock formation, Foundation of the Gods: Rock and Waterscapes systems Inc. Painted sky: Sky Art. Store face finish, supplier of 'Duroplex' product: Triarch Industries Inc.

Friedrichstadt Passagen – Quartier 205
Berlin, Germany
Architect: Prof. O. M. Ungers
Client: Tishman Speyer Properties Deutschland GmbH. Project Team: Prof. Karl-Heinz Winkens, Sebastian Klatt, Robert Beyer, Hugo Daiber, Angela Leonhardt, Tobias Scheel, Birgit Schindler, Tanya Trevisan, Martin Weisser. General Contractors: Steiner Infratec GmbH. Structural Planning: Ingenieurbüro für Bauwesen Prof. Dr.-Ing. Polonyi & Partner. Engineers: Jaros Baum & Bolles Consulting Engineers.

Friedrichstadt Passagen – Quartier 206
Architect: Pei Cobb Freed & Partners
Client: Jagdfeld Friedrichstadt Passagen Q 206. Project Team: Henry Cobb (Partner for Design); George Miller (Partner for Management), Theodore Musho (Associate Partner, Design), Brian McNally (Associate Partner, Management), Fritz Sulzer (façade technicque). Contact Architect: Arge Niedballa Grhl Hein. Structural Design: Prof. Polonyi und Fink GmbH. Mechanical Design: Jaros Baum & Bolles. Contractor: Dyckerhoff & Widmann. Client's Project Manager: Kappes Scholtz. Interiors: AMJ Holdings; Corso Como. Exterior Stone: Max Balz GmbH & Co. Interior Stone: Technostone: Vezzano Ligure.

Georges
Melbourne, Australia
Architect: Daryl Jackson Architects
Interior Designers: Daryl Jackson Interiors / Conran Design Partnership
Client: Georges Melbourne. Project Team: Daryl Jackson, Peter Quigley, Bill Ryan, Brian Richards, John O'Neill. Interior Design Team: Jane Mackay (DJI); Geraldine Maher (DJI), Hamish Guthrie (DJI), Olivia Jackson (DJI), Kate Hart (DJI), Jane Lawrence (CDP), Bridgit Salter (CDP). Project Management: Case Meallin & Associates. Builder: Probuild Constructions. Sub-contractors: PFC Shopfitting; Ramvek Shopfitting; S&B Shopfitting; Plaza Interiors; Allgood Interiors; Classic Resources; Elecraft. Lighting Consultant: Lighting Design Partnership. Lighting: Modular; Erco. Flooring: Domus Ceramics; Ground Kirkstone; Roger Sellers Myhill, Insernia Limestone; Bluestone Bamstone; Natural Image Products. Display Units: Ramvek Shopfitting; S&B Shopfitting;

Allgood Interiors; Classic Resources. Upholstery: Insuede, Instyle; Elmo Rustico; Warwick Fabrics. Glass Atrium and Central Staircase: Ahearn Metal Specialists. Signage: Hoyne Design in collaboration with CD Partnership.

Halfords Auto Depot
Swansea, Wales, UK
Interior Designer: Ben Kelly Design
Client: Halfords Ltd. Project Team: Patrick McKinney, Richard Blurton. Building Consultants, Project Management, Structural Engineers: BDN (Building Design Northern). Main Contractor: Stainforth Construction. Graphics/signage and branding: Lippa Pearce. Shopfitters: Gibson Lea. Electrical Contractor: Electec Services Ltd. Heating and Air Conditioning Engineers: Intherm.

HEP FIVE
Osaka, Japan
Architect: Takenaka Corporation
Main Contractors: Takenaka Corporation; Obayashi Corporation; Mori-Gumi Co. Ltd. Lighting Design: Uchihara Creative Lighting Design; Ushio Specs. Atrium Director: Tatsuya Ishii. Exterior Watt Art: Tatsuo Uchinami. Signage: Mishima Design.

Hushush
Tokyo, Japan
Interior Designer: Harry Allen & Associates
Designer: Harry Allen. Project Designer: Shawn Booth. Design Firm: KAZ Design Office New York & Osaka. Architect and Contractor: Sogo Design Co. Ltd.

Joseph Menswear
London, UK
Architect/Interior Designer: David Chipperfield Architects
Client: Joseph Ltd. Project Team: David Chipperfield, Patrick McInerney, An Fonteyne. Structural Engineer: Dewhurst MacFarlane. Quantity Surveyor: Time Gatehouse. Services: BDSP Partnership. Lighting: Isometrix. Stone Floor: Stoneage.

Alan Journo
Milan, Italy
Interior Designer: Ron Arad Associates
Client: Alan Journo. Project Team: Ron Arad, Barnaby Gunning, Kit Lewis, Elliot Howes, Dan Dorell. Site Architect: Giancarlo Conti. Project Management: Alan Journo. Specialist Metalwork: Marzorati Ronchetti.

Levi's Flagship Store, Regent Street
London, UK
Interior Designer: Checkland Kinleysides
Client: Levi Strauss UK. Project Team: Jeff Kindlysides, Jason West, Kathryn Deverill, Jill Summerfield, Carl Murch, Lee Draycott. Collaborating Designer: Into Lighting. Lighting: Into Lighting. Audio Visual: Vision RE. Mechanical & Electrical: Ian Williams Associates. Shopfitters: Barker Interiors. Suppliers: Drawn Metal Co (shopfront); Flowcrete (flooring); Niagra by Potter & Soar Ltd. (steel woven mesh);

Arch Fabrications (ballustrading, DJ Tower, gantry, uprights and ceiling rafters); Vision Re. Ltd (video equipment and projectors).

Lust for Life
Aachen, Germany
Architect: Kister Scheithauer Gross.
Interior Designer: Umdasch Shop-Concept
Client: Lust for Life – Magnus Swaczyna, Patrick C. M. Schalkwijk. Project Team: Wolfgang Strobl; Gunther Berger; Elke Bachlmair; Team ZED (concept); Matthias Meisel, Karin Kuhling, Team Meisel (realization). Lighting: Lust for Life.

Millennium Center
Budapest, Hungary
Interior Designer: Mahmoudieh Design
Client: Girocredit. Project Team: Jasmine Mahmoudieh, Albino Cipriani, Katrin Bollmann. Collaborating Architect: Prof. Finta. Main Contractors: Ed Ast & Co; Universale Internationale. Lighting Concpet: Mahmoudieh Design. Lighting Consultant: Gert Pfarre. Original roof: Gustave Eiffel. Restoration of Millenium Centre: Dr. Finta.

Herman Miller Showroom
Chicago, Illinois, USA
Interior Designer: Krueck & Sexton Architects
Client: Herman Miller Inc. Project Team: Mark Sexton, Robin Johnson, Tom Jacobs (Project architects). Main Contractor: Clune Construction Company. Product Display: Environment Group. Lighting: Schuller & Shook; John Boesche Design. Graphics: Thirst; Joyce Mast Graphic Design. Specialities: Xibitz Inc. Engineering: McGuire Engineers, Engineering Consultants. Millwork: Parenti & Raffaelli. Metal Panels: Rigidized Metals Corporation. Glass: Trainor Glass. Sandblasting Glass: Skyline Design. Slumped Glass: Ultra Glass. Custom Metalwork: Tesko Enterprises. Drywall: Tempes Construction. Terrazzo Work: Metropolitan Terrazzo. Carpet: Interface Flooring Systems. Painting: Ascher Brothers. Curtains: North-west Drapery Services. Ductwork: Hill Mechanical Group. Electrical: Continental Electrical Construction Co.

More Moss
New York, New York, USA
Interior Designer: Harry Allen & Associates
Client: M. W. Moss. Project Team: Harry Allen, Shawn Booth. Main Contractor: Blake Addison. Structural Engineer: Hage Engineering. Electrician: Walford Electrical. Metal work: Dominic Minervini of Artistic Metal Works. Cabinetry and laminate work: Ladislav Czernek of Epoche Studio. Glass: James Huddleston of Penta-Glass Industries Inc.

Moschino
London, UK
Interior Designer: Hosker Moore & Kent
Client: Moshino. Project Team: Peter Kent (Partner), Rachel Toomey. Shopfitter: Charles Barrett. Flooring: Unifloor SRL. Lighting: Modular. Signage: Studio.

Credits

Graphics: Moschino application by ABC Graphics. Special Features: Verburg & Brownfield (polished bronze door handles); Propshop (silver rain curtain and rain chandelier).

Munich Airport Center
Munich, Germany
Architect: Murphy/Jahn
Client: Flughafen Munich GmbH; MFG Delta KG, Alba GmbH. Project Team: Helmut Jahn, Sam Scaccia, Rainer Schildknecht, Steven Cook, Charles Bostick, Steven Nilles, John Myefski. Mechanical Engineer: HL-Technik AG. Structural Engineer: Grebner Beratende Ingenieure GmbH. Structural Engineer (roof): Ove Arup & Partners. Landscape Architects: Peter Walker & Partners; Prof. Rainer Schmidt; Wolfgang Roth; RWDI – Rower Williams. Wind Tunnel Consultants: Davies & Irwin Inc. Curtainwall Consultant: Ingenieurburo Schaim GmbH & Co. KG.

Nike Town
London, UK
Interior Designer: BDP Design; Nike Retail Design
Client: Nike Retail bv. Project Team: Nick Terry (Project Director BDP), Martin Cook (Interior Design and Managing Director BDP), Stephen Anderson (Project Design Team Leader, BDP Design Director), Jack Hobbs (Project Team Leader, BDP Design Director), Sarah Turnbill, Rachel Brown, Grego Holme. Associate Designers: Electrosonic Ltd. (audi-visual); Main Contractor: Kvaerner Trollope and Colls. Building services: Lorne Stewart. Metalwork and Joinery: Trollope Colls Elliott. Theatrical lighting: AC Lighting. Partitioning: Boler and Clarke. Stock storage system: Penwright. Stock transport system (shoe tubes): Telelift (UK) Ltd. Suspended ceilings: James Rose Projects Ltd. Clock Feature: John Smith. Plaster: Armourcoat. Epoxy resin terrazzo floors: Fribel International. Rubber flooring: Dalsouple. Aluminium grate flooring: Eurotech. Paving: Charcon. Lighting: Concord.

Pakhuis
Amsterdam, The Netherlands
Architect / Interior Designer: Meyer en van Schooten Architects
Client: Pakhuis Amsterdam BV. Project Team: Roberto Meyer, Jeroen van Schooten, Felix van Bemmel, May Kooreman, Erik Jan Vermeulen. Quality supervisor: Meyer en van Schooten Architects BV; Interim Bouwconsult BV. Structural Advisor: Adviesburo voor BouwTechniek BV. Contractor: Bouwbedrijf EA van den Hengel BV. Electrical Contractor: E.T.B. Cas Sombroek BV. Mechanical Contractor: Wolter en Drox Groep. Sprinklers: Unica Installatietechniek BV.

Promenaden Hauptbahnhof
Leipzig, Germany
Architect: ECE Projektmanagement GmbH & Co. KG
Client: BME-Bahnhof Management und Entwicklungsgesellschaft mbH. General Planning: ECE Projektmanagement GmbH & Co. KG in collaboration with Architekten HPP Hentrich-Petschnigg & Partner KG. General Management: J. Faust, H. Henkel, R. Thoma, H.J. Stutz, M. Zotter. Project Management: W. Sübai, U. Wittner. Project Team: M. Röhr, S. Kampen, S. Wiegsandt, K. Schmidt, U. Schnorr, J. Benning, C. Reissner, L. Allert, G. Scherner, T. Rasche, A. Leschinger, A. Schwab, H. Pedina, H. Mührmann. General Builder: Walter Bau AG. Refurbishment of Train Hall: Ingenieurbüro Schmitt-Stumph-Frühauf.

Pronovias
Madrid, Spain
Interior Designer: GCA Arquitectos
Client: Pronovias SA. Project Team: Josep Juanpere (Architect), Sandra Vidal. Main Contractor: Codecsa SA. Furniture: GCA Arquitectos (design); Ebanisteria Pomar (manufacture). Carpet: Alterra. Track lighting: Claris by Mobles 114. Floor lamp: Stylos by Flos.

Publix on the Bay
Miami Beach, Florida, USA
Architect: Wood and Zapata
Client: Publix Supermarkets Inc. Project Team: Carlos Zapata, Benjamin T. Wood (Principals in Charge); Wyatt Porter-Brown, Victoria Steven, Fred Botelho, Eric Klingler, Rolando Mendoza, Anthony Montalto, Pamela Torres; Melissa Koff (Project Co-ordination). General Contractor: Keene Construction. Structural Engineer: Leslie E Robertson Associates. MEP Engineer: Thomas Engineering. Civil Engineering: Bermello, Ajamil & Partner. Landscape Architect: Rosenberg Design Group.

Rüsing und Rüsing
Düsseldorf, Germany
Architect: Torsten Neeland
Client: Bernhard Rüsing. Design Team: Vincent Hewitt, Mark Frankland, Sandra Thomsen. Cabinet Maker: Benno Meuthen, Meuthen GmbH. Floor: Käser GmbH & Co.KG. Lighting (corridor): Kreon. Light Cubes: Der Kluth. Lichtsteuerung Lighting: Erco Leuchten GmbH. Interactive Media (conference room): G+B Medientechnik GmbH. Electrician: Klaus Cyrys.

Selfridges, Trafford Centre
Manchester, UK
Architect: Chapman Taylor Partners
Interior Designers: John Herbert Partnership / Conran Design Partnership / Gerald Taylor, Aldo Cibic
Client: Selfridges. John Herbert Partnership Project Team: James Herbert (Project Leader). Implementation Architects: Leache Rhodes Walker. Aldo Cibic Project Team: Nick Perie; Gerald Taylor. Main Contractor: Bovis. Engineers: Oscar Faber. Quantity Surveyors: Parker & Browne. Project Management: Clarson Goff Management. Peel Holdings plc Implementation Architect: Leache Rhodes Walker. Quantity Surveyor: Deacon & Jones. Structural/Civil Engineer: Bingham Cotterell & Partners. Building Service Engineer: WSP Consulting Engineers. Landscape Architects: Derek Lovejoy Partnership. Traffic Engineer: TPK Partnership. Management Contractor: Bovis Europe. The Orient Theme Designer: The Building A Theme Co. Ltd. Lighting Consultant: Theo Londos. Interior Landscaping: MESA. Graphics & Signage: Chapman Taylor Partners.

Sirius Smart Sounds
Maastricht, The Netherlands
Architect: Maurice Mentjens
Client: Sirius VOF. Project Team: Maurice Mentjens, Johan Gielissen, Chequita Nahar with Mathijs de Ponti, Roland Manders, Lisa Diephuys, Erwin Theunissen. Floor covering: Borchert Systhemen Landgraaf. Metal Supplier: Ameco Vanlo. Polished by: Altena BV. Electrical Installation: Gaby Armino. Painting: Arie Winterink.

Superga
Madrid, Spain
Architect: Studio Iosa Ghini
Client: Superga. Contractor and supplier: Lisar.

Swatch Timeship
New York, New York, USA
Architect: Pentagram Design
Client: Swatch. Project Team: James Biber, Daniel Weil. General Contractor: Richter & Ratner. Patterned Stainless Steel: Rigidized Metal by Armore Metals. Cabinet fabrication: Rathe Productions. Epoxy terrazzo floor: D. Magnam & Co. Storefront: Precision Glass. Glass: Bendheim. Lights: Johnson Schwinghammer; Litelab. Pneumatic Tube System: ATC. Railings: Blumcraft. Countertops: Dlubak Custom Fabricated Glass. Stools: L&B Seating. Letter/7 Segment Display: Signalex. Paintwork: Benjamin Moore. Laminates: Abet Laminate; Mettle Mica. Watch Graphic: 3M.

Vasco da Gama
Lisbon, Portugal
Architect: Building Design Partnership (BDP)
Client: Sonae Imobilaria. Project Team: Peter Shuttleworth (Architect, Director), Terry Davenport (Architect, Director), Dan Smyth (Associate Architect). Collaborating Designer: Jose Quintela de Fonseca, Sonae Imobillaria. Retail outlets: Promontorio Architect. M&E Engineers: LMA. Project Management: Engexpor Project Managers.

Virmani Fashion Shop
Munich, Germany
Architect: Design Associates
Client: Virmani Pradeep. Project Team: Stephan Lang, Uwe Binnberg. Main Contractor: Schreinerei Eham. Lighting: Catallani and Smith; Kreon.

Warenhuis Vanderveen
Assen, The Netherlands
Architect: Architectuurstudio Herman Hertzberger
Client: Warenhuis Vanderveen, Koopmansplein. Project Team: Herman Hertzberger, Willemvan Winsen, Folkert Stropsma, Arienne Matser, Cor

Credits

Kruter, Laurens Jan ten Kate, Andrew Dawes. Main Contractor: Vosbouw BV. Structural Engineer: Ingenieursbureau Wassenaar BV. Services Consultant: IHN Groningen. Heating and Sanitation: Luc. Alkema. Sanitary Facilities: Alkema. Steel Construction: Winel. Steel: Machinefabriek Rinsma. Front Construction: Aluminium Gevels en Glastechniek Wemmenhove. Paintwork: Max Manmak. Concrete Construction: Betonbouw Drenthe. Glass: Asser Glas-en Verfhandel. Electrics: Elektrotechnische Groothandel Voskampen Dijkstra.

Waterstone's Piccadilly
London, UK
Interior Designer: BDG McColl
Layout: Waterstone's
Architect: John Strong & Partners
Client: Waterstone's. Main Contractor: Withey Contracts Ltd. Project Manager: Project Solutions. Planning Architects: John Strong & Partners. Contractor for Searcy's Bars and Restaurants: Kiddies Contractors.

Win a Cow Free
Tokyo, Japan
Concept Planner: Setsumasa Kobashi
Constructor: D-BRAIN.

Zero Lustrum Pukeberg
Stockholm, Sweden
Interior Designer: Rupert Gardner Design
Client: Andris Nolendorfs. Builder: Olle Sahlens Bygg & Projektlednings AB. Interior Carpentry/Woodwork: Eriksdals Snickeri AB. Glass and Metalwork: Nybergs Glas & Metall AB. Tile and Mosaic: Enskede Parkett & Kakel AB. Stone Floor: Stenfirma Bror Torner AB. Light and Panel Tracks: Hawa Sverige AB.

Zumtobel Staff Lichtzentrum
Berlin, Germany
Architects: Sauerbruch Hutton Architekten.
Client: Zumtobel Licht GmbH. Project Team: Matthias Sauerbruch, Louisa Hutton, Fredrik Kallstrom, Andrea Frensch, Jan Laufer. Structure: Leonard Andra und Partner. Services: Bohne Ingenieure. Paintwork: Herr Schlewinski; Herr Rockstreh; Jastra. Metalwork: Jastra. Light deck: Kluth. Dry course/woodwork: Bley. Floor covering: Pre We Na GmbH; Schuh; Botex. Electrical work: Zumtobel. Building surveyor/brickwork: Bielsen Bauchemie. Carpentry: Biermann und Knoop. Plasterwork: Weck und Linke. Locksmith: Jastra.

Photo Credits

The author and the publishers would like to thank all the designers and architects involved and the photographers whose work is reproduced. The following photographic credits are given, with page numbers in parentheses:

Jon Arnold (38–41); Gunter Bieringer (cover, 122–5); Bielenberg (202–204); bitter-bredt, berlin (24–29); Richard Bryant/Arcaid (88–91); Courtesy Caesar's Palace (162–5); Niall Clutton (30–33); Santi Caleca (118–121); Wilfried Dechau (178–181); Jan Derwig (52–3, 54 right); Peter Durant/arcblue (134–5); ECE Projektmanagement (182–7); Engellhardt/Sellin (188–191); Elizabeth Felicella (92); Klaus Frahm/artur (68–73); Raphaël Franco (210–13); Denis Gilbert (137); Richard Glover (84–6); Jeff Goldberg/Esto (148–153); Brigida Gonzales (175); Roland Halbe/artur (138–9); Robin A. Head (106–111); Hedrich Blessing (13–19), Tim Hursley (200–201, 205); Werner Huthmacher (56–61); Arthur Hunt (42–7); Bert Janssen (102–105); Krishna Lahote (174, 176–7); Ian Lawson (218–19); Nathaniel Lieberman (142–3); Ake E:Son Lindman AB (113, 116–17); Duccio Malagamba (206–209); Peter Mauss/Esto (48–51); Ian McKinnell (222–7)Trevor Mein (214–17); Jordi Miralles (96–101); James Morris (20–23), Osamu Murai (159–161); Nacasa & Partners (2, 63–7, 74–9, 126–131); Jon O'Brien (220–221); Michael Perlmutter (112, 114); Christian Richters (193–9); Pinto Rosales (34–7); P. Ruault (166–9); A. Rusov (80-83); Shinkenchiku-sha (158); Rue Morais de Sousa (144–7); Andrew Southall/arcblue (136); Markus Tollhopf (154–7); Fritz van Dijk (54 left); Morley von Sternberg (170–73); Michael Weschler (93–4).

Index

Acknowledgements
The author and co-ordinating researcher would like to
thank Robert Thiemann for his helpful information,
Susan Lawson for her kind assistance in research and
Paul Harron for his patience in editing this book – they also
give a warm welcome to his son Angus, who was born
during the collaboration.